architecture

projects and architecture
DOMINIQUE PERRAULT
with an essay by laurent stalder

Electaarchitecture

Editor
Giovanna Crespi

Copy Editor
Gail Swerling

Translation
Christopher Evans

Distributed by Phaidon Press
ISBN 1-904313-03-5

www.electaweb.it

Contents

7   Architeture: Projection of the Mind and Protection of the Body
Laurent Stalder

Works and Projects
28   Hôtel Industriel Jean-Baptiste Berlier, Paris
32   IRSID, Usinor-Sacilor Convention Center, Saint-Germain-en-Laye
36   Bibliothèque Nationale de France, Paris
46   Olympic Velodrome and Swimming Pool, Berlin
54   Centre Technique du Livre, Bussy Saint-Georges
58   La Grande Serre, La Villette, Paris
62   Plan of Reclamation of the Unimetal Area, Caen
68   Enlargement of the Court of Justice of the European Union, Luxembourg
72   Aplix Factory, Le Cellier-sur-Loire
76   Mediathèque, Vénissieux
80   Urban Development Scheme and Sports Facilities, Badalona
84   Landscaping Project for the Temple of Mithras, Naples
86   Competition for an Urban Park in the Falck Area, Sesto San Giovanni
92   Competition for Convention Center at the EUR, Rome
94   Competition for the Layout of Piazza Gramsci, Cinisello Balsamo
98   Competition for the New Seat of the University College of Architecture
       in the Area of the Former Cold-Storage Facilities, San Basilio, Venice
102   Competition Project for the Citadel of Justice, Salerno
106   Competition for the City of Culture, Santiago de Compostela
112   Competition for the New Consiag Office Building, Prato
116   M-Preis Supermarket, Wattens
120   "Milano 2001" Competition for an Illuminated Sign, Milan
122   Competition Project for the Enlargement of the Galleria Nazionale
       d'Arte Moderna, Rome

Design
with Gaëlle Lauriot-Prévost
128   Furniture for the Bibliothèque Nationale de France
134   Metal Furnishings

137   **Chronology of Works**

Appendices
177   Biography
178   Bibliography
179   Composition of the Studio Dominique Perrault, Architect
179   References

Architecture: Projection of the Mind and Protection of the Body

Laurent Stalder

"*La mort de l'architecture*"[1]—so Perrault is looking forward to the death of architecture. The discipline has failed and, unlike in other fields, its representatives have never dared declare its bankruptcy. The breaking of rules in painting has signified an active participation "in this death of art," just as quantum mechanics has been "a declaration of death" for classical physics. Over the course of the twentieth century only architecture has failed to notice and proclaim its own death. It has got tangled up in the aesthetic and cultural coils of the principles of modernity and shut itself up in its own narrow sphere. Dominique Perrault's criticisms of architecture are merciless. "It is absolutely necessary to abandon the traditional field of architecture, to extend it to other realms, in order to go beyond its constituted language, to proceed by grafts, artificial insemination."[2] Here he is referring not so much to the essence of the discipline as to its methodical approach. Naturally, in order to carry out these "grafts" and this "insemination," with the aim of setting architecture free from its self-contained discourse, he looks back to the artistic currents of the late sixties, i.e. to those disciplines that had proclaimed the "death of art"—and obviously its rebirth as well. The systematic separation of the conceptual phase from the executive one—to the point where the latter is even spurned—has led to a substantial clarification of the process of design. In his first manifesto, the *Paragraphs on Conceptual Art*, Sol LeWitt put it in these pregnant terms: "In conceptual art the idea of concept is the most important aspect of the work. When the artist uses a conceptual form of art, it means that all of the planning and decisions are made beforehand and the execution is a perfunctory affair."[3] Although Sol LeWitt naturally clings to the sharp distinction between art and architecture—the first is pure idea, the second is linked to practical aims—the method and instruments he uses are essentially architectural: "The idea itself, even if not made visual, is as much a work of art as any finished product. All intervening steps—scribbles, sketches, drawings, failed work, models, studies, thought, conversations—are of interest. Those that show the thought process of the artist are sometimes more interesting than the final product."[4]

So the flight from the discipline postulated by Perrault is at the same time a return to the wellspring of the discipline itself. When Perrault defines architecture as "projection of the mind and protection of the body,"[5] he is alluding not just to the opposition between idea and matter, intellectual work and manual work, emphasized by Sol LeWitt, but also to one of the oldest *topoi* in the history of architecture: "*Ea [architecti scientia] nascitur ex fabrica et ratiocinatione*" ("It [the science of the architect] stems from manual and intellectual work"). Even where Perrault, speaking of "grafts" and "insemination," calls for other disciplines to be taken into account, he is in no way departing from the Vitruvian principle that "the cultural contributions of many sciences and experience of the other arts go into the preparation of the architect [...]."[6]

All this serves to define the approach that will be taken here, where the aim cannot of course be to interpret the architectural work of Dominique Perrault from a historical perspective. Rather, an attempt will be made to identify along general lines the theoretical and architectural problems of a career characterized by "grafts" and "insemination," partly of a historical type.

*Dominique
Perrault, Olympic
swimming pool,
Berlin.*

8

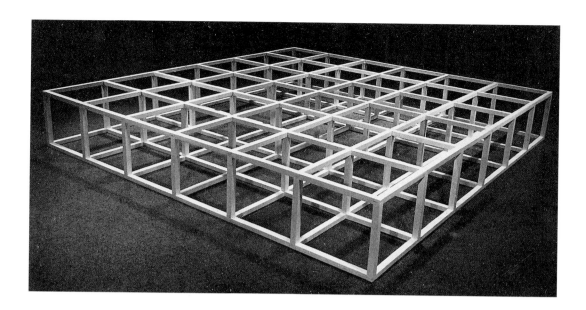

It is precisely where he brings into question not so much the essence of architecture as its methods, not so much the discipline as such as its conventions, that it seems most opportune to investigate the fundamental problems of his creative process. So the work as realized has to be considered together with the relative design phase. The author is conscious of running a twofold risk: that of producing, with an argument structured in too systematic a way, an unsatisfactory theoretical construction or, vice versa, that of fragmenting his output in a thematic description. But this introduction to the works of Dominique Perrault aims not so much to have the last word on the matter as to familiarize readers with what the architect has done without limiting their freedom, an indispensable presupposition for an open mind.

"Architecture, Projection of the Mind"

The architect is "he who with sure and perfect method is able to rationally design and practically realize [...] works that meet the most important needs of man in the best way possible."[7] Alberti lists in chronological order the means of "definition" to which the architect resorts in the creative process. While the drawing in its abstraction and generality comes the closest to the idea, the model, as an anticipation of reality, serves to verify the building and its parts before constructing it. Thus he fixes the hierarchical succession of the most important phases of the passage from theory to practice.

The terms "concept" and "process," also employed by Dominique Perrault, refer essentially to the same thing. The former is the "projection of the mind" or "the idea."[8] It represents a declaration of intent: "overlaying," "preserving," "including," "hybridizing," etc.[9] The latter, "working concept" or "accompanying idea,"[10] indicates the various phases that follow one another from the conception to its material translation.

But these stages in the architectural process are no longer separated in a preestablished and idealized sequence. On the contrary: "The work has to be carried out simultaneously in all the dimensions of the process and it is necessary to re-create tools, a language, more adequate responses for each project."[11] This open-minded attitude is reflected in the figurative means employed. Depending on the program, the client and the phase of design, models and pictures of models, retouched photographs and sketches, computer images, collages, diagrams, etc. are applied simultaneously. In publications these different means are given the same importance as photographs of the building under construction and images of the whole or details of the completed building. Creative process and finished work are placed on the same level.

Constant factors of great significance can be found in these types of figuration. In the majority of the projects the sketch is the most precise reproduction of the idea on paper and often reflects

9

the analytical process: "a chair + a chair for reading = a reading chair" or "the castle + the glass disk = the duplicate of the castle."[12] The sketch is abstract, free from the constraints of the context and the material. It does not represent a reflection of fleeting thoughts or a line of research, but the result of that research.

The other figurative means are functional to the process of design. They present details that are gradually combined to produce a many-sided, ever-changing image of the project itself. Their fragmentary nature needs to be emphasized. The associative force of the collage, the material concreteness of models, the conceptual value of the sketch, the persuasive character of diagrams and the precise effect of particular choices make it possible to put across much of the message without fixing it definitively. This results in a loss not only of the hierarchy between drawing and sketch, between drawing and model, but also between sample of materials and model. Even though the means used attain a high degree of precision and can prefigure individual aspects with great accuracy, they also leave ample margins for free perception.

It is only in this way that the "idealistic vision of the architectural project,"[13] the predefined succession of the individual phases of design and their separation from the process of construction, can be brought into question: "The separation between conception and realization is blurred."[14] If the idea anticipates the process of construction, it is also true that the latter conditions the project itself. It is no coincidence that the Aplix factory was already under construction when its façade was designed. In the Bibliothèque Nationale de France the static structures were even chosen in such a way as to allow him to go on revising the design during construction and to make changes to the uses to which it would be put *a posteriori*. Design, realization, utilization and their possible alterations proceed in parallel in the chronological succession. But in this way the finished building is no longer a compositional unity, but a unitary state within a process of evolution. In this context it is worth mentioning the project for the redevelopment of the Unimetal industrial area at Caen. Here project and execution overlap and it is hard to distinguish between them. It is not a project for construction that is in the foreground, but the devising of a strategy for the future use of the area: "defining what the future might be."[15] While collages and photomontages, with their allusive references, can illustrate the character of the site and the possible interventions in a very precise way, drawing attention to or decontextualizing what already exists, the measures taken, such as the breakdown of the area into a grid of roads, reveal the characteris-

*The site of the
project for the
Unimetal area,
Caen.*

tics of a model. Consequently the "first environmental propositions"[16] are much more binding than the grid realized. This is simply a form of organization that indicates property rights and the size of lots, but is able to say little about the future image, since "progressively, inscribing themselves over time, the programs, unknown today, will take their place."[17] It is just here that the open method of design which permits individual phases to exist one alongside the other without limiting one another proves essential.

The architect is "he who with sure and perfect method is able to rationally design and practically realize [...] works." The fact that architecture is an intellectual act is demonstrated in a self-evident manner by the sketches that fix the idea. At the same time, however, the figurative means, the models, the drawings and to some extent even the interventions on the ground show on the one hand that it is no longer possible to follow the individual phases of the architectural process in a linear way, and on the other that even the structures built can remain fragmentary and merely have the character of a model. Designing is in fact "this notion of process, of operation."[18]

"The Language of Man"

If the sketch is a representation of the idea and if the various models can prefigure aspects of reality, the precise architectural drawing remains, thanks to the systematic nature of its geometry, the sole language that, on the strength of its scientific nature, is capable of translating the project into a constructed work. Like language, geometry is a product of the human intellectual faculty. It is a reflection of the ability to formulate an abstract thought, but also a means of creating order—"*mettre en place*"—and fixing dimensions—"*capter*."[19] It serves to subject what lacks discipline to systematic understanding. So geometry is at once means and method, representation and foundation of architecture.

Geometry is essential in Perrault's work. The grid, which is used to explore and measure the site and is generally square, constitutes the geometric foundation of numerous projects. At Caen it is 100 by 100 meters, and on the Falck site it has roughly the same dimensions. The area of the Aplix factory is subdivided into units of 22 by 22 meters. In Venice the paving measures 4.5 by 4.5 meters. The supports that hold up the circular plate of the convention centre of Usinor-Sacilor are square. The pattern outlined by the supports of the Mithraeum in Naples is also based on the square and even the panes of the windows of the Bibliothèque Nationale de France or the Hôtel Industriel Berlier have dimensions of 1:2.

The complex of the Aplix factory is presented in accordance with the "strict rules of geometry and of the syntax of a crossword grid."[20] This is not a description of the architectural structure, but just of the rules that underpin it. The compositional or aesthetic-formal choices are not mentioned, but the combinatorial standards that preside over the different phases of production and the successive enlargement of the layout are discussed. On the basis of these characteristics, the various production phases are fitted together, "as letters form words."[21] So it is possible to add the "elementary elements" without violating the fundamental principle, the only one to establish the rigorous organization of the geometric grid and its division into squares according to a scheme of aseptic neutrality. On the other hand the scale of the mesh and the utilization of the squares, related to the requirements of a standardized model of business administration, are not defined. The grid also fixes the undeterminable future expansion of the factory. This programmatic flexibility is elevated to an "aesthetic principle producing an undetermined architectural form."[22] Thus the grid constitutes not just the structure of the project proper, but also lays down the rules of a subsequent evolution, not determinable for the moment. The grid is at once the structure and the method of the architectural idea. And inevitably it is also the generating principle of the form.

Notwithstanding this peculiarity, the grid remains a methodological aid that cannot take the place of the idea behind the design. In the development of the Falck area in Milan, the "binary grid, in the likeness of a checkerboard," is explicitly described as "an elastic, open and flexible method of realization," subordinate to the idea "of creating/conjuring up a park in the heart of the city." However, the checkerboard pattern does make it possible to give a precise form to the urbanistic intention of "developing the city with its streets, avenues, blocks of buildings and squares with their gardens, with the aim of linking the southern districts with the northern ones, the western districts with the eastern ones," and of carrying out this project in stages, in a flexible but coherent way: "one square after another."[23] Thus the interposed structure delineates a new order within the preexistent ones. The width of the mesh is chosen in such a way as to meet

the specific needs of the idea. Hence it permits on the one hand the size of the blocks to match the existing layouts and on the other assigns the desired principle of organization to the open park. It is only through the idea that the structure is given sense and meaning.

Method and concept are not always so easy to distinguish. In the proposal for the park to be laid out in the Falck area they are almost inextricable. Here a significant part is played by the history of the place, given that the vegetation is not regarded simply as "material composing the architecture of the city," i.e. as a traditional area of greenery, but "nature treated as an industrial component along the lines of the aircraft parts […] once made at the Falck factories." The basic idea consists in the illustration of an industrial process, the mirroring of a production cycle. Just as the preserved industrial ruins are translated into their fundamental geometric elements— point (tower), line (conveyer belt), area and mass (buildings)—the vegetation is distinguished into point (pines, oaks), line (poplars, limes), area (lawns, lily ponds) and mass (bamboo grove). The subdivision into four types corresponds to the rules of the grid. In this way two adjoining spaces never have the same type of vegetation. And so the order that underlies the whole always remains comprehensible. The rigid coherence of the method is attenuated by the fact that the different densities, heights, cycles and growth patterns of the plants guarantee, together with the surviving industrial plant and the preexisting areas of greenery, the necessary variety and alternation.

The description of the intervention as an "act of contemporary art" and "act of Land Art"[24] is significant, but what is interesting in this project is the systematic procedure. In the field of conceptual art Mel Bochner has studied the characteristics of serial organization, a category which includes the grid: "Serial order is a method, not a style. The results of this method are surprising and diverse. […] The serial attitude is a concern with how order of a specific type is manifest."[25] Bochner has pointed out, in analogy with linguistics, that this principle of order is self-referential. So it has no other significance than its own conformity to the rule. A definition that does not admit different interpretations, such as the one provided for the Falck area, where there is a clear reference to industrial production. What emerges here are the differences between art and architecture highlighted over the same period by Sol LeWitt in his "Paragraphs on Conceptual Art": "Architecture, whether it is a work of art or not, must be utilitarian or else fail completely. Art is not utilitarian. When three-dimensional art starts to take on some of the characteristics of architecture such as forming utilitarian areas it weakens its function as art."[26]

But it is in the design of the park that the "elastic, open and flexible method of realization" is fused with the systematic representation of "nature treated as an industrial component." Although the "evocations of history," "traces on the ground," chance and the cycle of nature, as well of course as the requirements of the program, all weaken the autonomy of the grid, this project shows that "investigation of architecture's capacity for abstraction"[27] represents the real challenge.

This challenge is one of the peculiar functions of architecture. The clear and at the same time undefined pattern of the grid has always made it an effective planning tool. It is only when it becomes visible that it acquires architectural significance. In the design of a roof for the Mithraeum in a square in the centre of Naples, three different grids are set one alongside the other: the orthogonal layout of the streets, the modular structure of the stonework of the ruined temple and the regular pattern of the supports of the new roof. It is only when they take on material form as blocks of houses, remains of walls and supports, performing their independent function linked to the size of the meshes, that they become distinguishable and take on meaning. Perrault has identified these properties by resorting to the concepts "*mettre en place*" (creating order) and "*capter*" (making perceptible through internal dimensions). An order can only be grasped if it is materialized in an architectural form. The grid has to be specific, and yet general at the same time: it is both the support and the thing supported. It was just this mutual interaction that Le Corbusier expressed so aptly when he observed "there was no other way in which [primitive man] could create something that gave him the impression of creating," going on to conclude: "Geometry is the language of man."[28]

"The Effect of Bodies"
The architectural grid, with its rigorous and systematic illustration during the design process, corresponds without a doubt to the concept of method for art outlined by Mel Bochner in his aforementioned essay. But at the moment of its translation into reality the differences pointed out by Sol LeWitt emerge, differences that are connected with the functional nature of architecture and its need to attain practical aims: "When the viewer is distracted by the large size of a piece this domination emphasizes the physical and emotive power of the form at the expense of losing the idea of the piece."[29] Sol LeWitt—leaving aside the contradiction inherent in his apology for the nonrepresentational in conceptual art—is referring here to one of the central peculiarities of classical architecture, and one that crops up continually. From Boullée's "effects of bodies"[30] to Le Corbusier's "higher emotion, of a mathematical order"[31] and Perrault's definition of the Bibliothèque Nationale as "the 'less is more' of emotion,"[32] the sensations aroused by architecture have always been closely bound up with the distinct forms of geometric bodies.

But does not this aspect, the emotional quality implicit in architecture, find an echo in Perrault's description of the velodrome and indoor swimming pool, a project with a markedly geometric character, constructed in Berlin: "What is the velodrome? It is a circle. The indoor swimming pool? A rectangle. That's all. In the last analysis I find that this assessment—the velodrome is round, the swimming pool rectangular—demonstrates better than anything else that architecture does not lie in the form. It is beyond it, outside it."[33] It is precisely for these buildings with a strongly determined function that it is not possible to consider the form an end in itself, but just the result of a design process. So does the form arise spontaneously from the fulfilment of the program? The circular plate of the ceiling that covers the elliptical track suggests that the question is more complex and cannot be reduced to a mere recipe deducible from functional considerations.

In effect the majority of Dominique Perrault's buildings are "simple bodies in geometrical terms."[34] They are assigned the qualities of "identity" and "unity." The point lies in trying to give them, in spite of their structural linearity, forms that are "as rich, complex, varied and flexible as possible."[35] Like the grid, the geometric body is primarily a methodological tool that creates a unifying order in which room can be found for different needs and for potential changes. Alongside the property of imparting order, therefore, emphasis is also placed on the aesthetic and formal one of the organic image.

Robert Morris, to whose *Mirrored Cubes* Perrault has compared the Bibliothèque Nationale,[36] tackles this question in his "Notes on Sculpture" and attributes "strong gestalt sensations" to simple bodies.[37] By this expression he is referring first of all to the possibility of perceiving them as organic figures from every point of view. But at the same time he is underlining the relationship between geometric forms and the effect they produce on the senses. Le Corbusier used the example of the Parthenon to clarify these qualities. In particular, he stressed architecture's

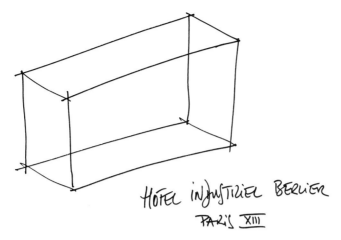

Dominique Perrault, Hôtel Industriel Jean-Baptiste Berlier, Paris, view and study sketch

HÔTEL INDUSTRIEL BERLIER
PARIS XIII

Le Corbusier, Vers une architecture: "La leçon de Rome: les volumes simples."

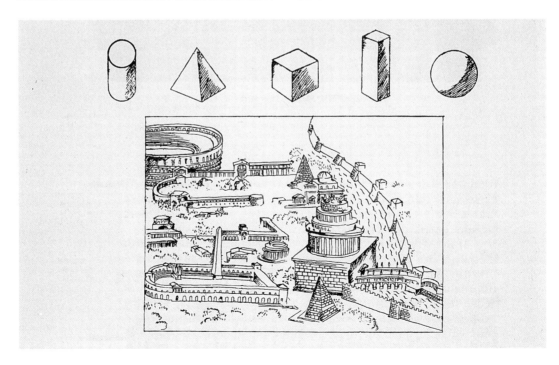

*Dominique
Perrault,
Bibliothèque
Nationale de
France, Paris.*

Amédée Ozenfant,
Les constantes:
horizontalité.

capacity to render an organizing idea tactile through its translation into material: "The Parthenon brings certainties: the higher emotion, of a mathematical order. Art is poetry."[38] "Emotion" is also the concept Perrault uses to describe the Bibliothèque Nationale, when he asserts "objects and their materials are nothing without the light that transcends them."[39] By this he is referring on the one hand to the elementary properties of geometry, the breadth of "horizontality," the linearity of "verticality,"[40] the coherence and identity of "simple bodies," and on the other to the "immediate and specific nature"[41] of the materials and their phenomenological qualities: "the intensity of the smelting"[42] of the metal, "that sort of incredible strength"[43] of the asphalt, but also the freshness of the fragrance of pine trees. Thus the field of "emotion" goes well beyond geometry. "Forms are certainly a part of architecture, but they don't explain it."[44] Here the circle is closed. Of course, simple geometric bodies do not in themselves constitute architecture. Nevertheless, as the methodological foundations of the project, they have organizational, aesthetic and formal qualities which must be taken into account in the design process. Emotion does not arise solely from the contemplation of two-dimensional patterns and the interplay of light and shade created by the illumination of three-dimensional bodies. Rather, it stems from a dynamic and continually changing perception of the phenomenological properties of architectural bodies along with their colors, materials and light effects. Only in this way can architecture completely fulfil the task set it: "to reach the brain without passing through the intellect."[45]

"The Emotion of the Meeting"
The artist Carl Andre has analyzed the distinction between form and structure, examining the history of sculpture in the twentieth century from a radical perspective. From a viewpoint that is not so much systematic as chronological, he sees it as a process that has led from sculpture as form to sculpture as structure to sculpture as place. In this way Andre has outlined the passage from the object imbued with iconographic content to the self-referential "figure" and all the way to the artifact which is connected to its location and capable of characterizing it. Andre has defined the place as "an area within an environment which has been altered in such a way as to make the general environment more conspicuous."[46] Although Andre also attributes sensorial qualities to his bodies, i.e. the requisites of form and material, he sees the value of contemporary art as lying in the relationship with the surrounding space and in the tendency to push the object into the background and focus instead on its setting.

When Perrault defines the Hôtel Industriel as "an almost nothing and an I-don't-know-what"[47] capable of modifying the place in which it stands, or explores in Berlin the "absence of architecture in the academic sense of the term."[48] or in connection with the project for the A 20 expressway speaks of a "non-project,"[49] he always has the same concept in mind. He considers the possibility of intervening in a given context in such a way as to clarify it, and thus not so much to give form to an object as to reveal the distinctive features of a certain place, to be a trait peculiar to architecture. In this sense the Hôtel Industriel is not really an architectural structure but a landmark on the Paris orbital. In the A 20 project, the invisibility of the intervention, with the renunciation of tangible measures of construction such as bridges and tunnels, and the most complete restoration possible of the violated landscape are elevated to the status of programmatic principles. The layout of the expressway simply has to follow the topographic lie of the land like an infinite line, made visible by the movement of the vehicles travelling on it. With this project Perrault precisely captures the character attributed by Andre to his creations: "Most of my works [...] have been ones that are in a way causeways—they cause you to make your way along them or around them or to move the spectator over them. They're like roads, but certainly not fixed point vistas."[50] On the one hand the work requires a dynamic perception on the part of the observer, just as Perrault postulates for his projects. On the other Andre, with the metaphor of the road, sees the work of art as the fulcrum of any intervention and the consequent need for a twofold perception: of the place and of the object.

The "realization" of an artifact is at once "creation" of a new object and "alteration" of the surroundings. This reciprocal action is described effectively in connection with the Usinor-Sacilor convention center: "By placing 'the castle on a platform of glass,' one defines an unmistakable place and an identifiable sign."[51] Even where, as in this case, we are dealing with a subterranean and not very visible intervention, there is still an interaction between object and place, an element that Perrault discusses in many of his writings: "however, the whole of this process of construction of the building rests on an encounter, often dazzling, between a concept and a context, between an idea and a place. This 'great moment,' this tangible meeting, is nothing but emotion."[52] Thus the realm of the emotional effects aroused by architecture is expanded even further. To the qualities of simple, geometric bodies and the material is added the clarifying effect of the intervention on its surroundings. The chronological separation and hierarchical ordering carried out by the artist on the basis of a historical vision are reabsorbed into the architectural project as complementary aspects: place, structure and form.

So the autonomous and self-referential figure is no longer sufficient for a conception of architecture as intervention in an open space. Only in dialectical relationship with the context can it find its full legitimization, as the description of the phases in the design of the Bibliothèque Nationale makes clear: "When I received the program of 300,000 square meters [...] I made a shape out of

Dominique Perrault, A 20 expressway, Brive-Montauban.

Carl Andre, Secant.

plasticine at the same time as the model of the site. I placed my piece of plasticine [on it] and told myself that if I built it like that, it would be a real monster, an opaque mass, a bunker." Even if the geometric body, taken by itself as a "shape made out of plasticine," were able to provoke those "gestalt sensations" mentioned by Morris, it became, once inserted in the "model of the site," "a real monster." "So I squashed my shape and all that remained were the four corners along with the multiple references that I leave to your imagination."[53] If at first it were a question of studying the relationship between an already defined environment and the simple volume designed to fulfil the needs of the program, later the goal became that of harmonizing the architectural act and the characteristics of the context. On another occasion Perrault saw this encounter as the real process of representation: reinforcement, reduction, change, fusion, etc. This process permits the geometric body to be turned into a precise form and the environment into a specific place. The idea of this duality of object and place is of central importance to an understanding of Perrault's architectural work.

The Bibliothèque Nationale project illustrates the possibilities of this interaction in all their complexity. In the text presenting the project to the competition the library's relationship with the surroundings is described as the "starting point for a total restructuring of this part of the 13th arrondissement" and as "a place that maintains the continuity of the succession of great empty spaces bordering on the Seine, such as Place de la Concorde, the Champs de Mars, the Invalides."[54] Thus the dual function of the Bibliothèque Nationale is defined: monument, i.e. an architectural body with four towers dominating an industrial area, and important monumental square in the series of open spaces along the banks of the Seine. The historic city is read, in the broadest sense of the word, in a topographic and typological rather than a historicist sense: "It is still necessary to take history into account, but as one datum among others, and what is decisive in this history is that it produces a geography of a certain kind."[55] But it is precisely thanks to the way certain topographic features are highlighted, to the insertion of the Bibliothèque Nationale in the succession of places rich in Parisian history—be they squares or monuments, such as Notre Dame with its twin spires or the Eiffel Tower—that the building acquires, on top of its mere phenomenological presence, a higher and symbolic significance that is reflected unequivocally in its definition as "a square for Paris, a library for France."[56] Linked by its internal principle to an overall urbanistic context, the library becomes a place of national importance, on a par with the Champ de Mars or Place de la Concorde.

The artistic means employed and the formal qualities are the same as the ones described by Louis-Etienne Boullée in his own project for a library: "It should not be presumed that the author of this project, describing the sublime image that the place in question will present, has had the intention of speaking of the art that he might use for the decoration of this monument. He assures you that it will come from its immensity."[57] In the Bibliothèque de France—just as in Boullée's library—this "immensity" is perceived not as an architectural mass but as an open space, owing to the presence of a gigantic square. By the concept of character, Boullée is referring to the same emotional qualities that, according to Sol LeWitt, diminish the force of the idea in art.

The design process, understood as interaction between idea and place, determines not just the construction of a new architectural object, but also the conscious transformation of a preexisting order in the place. This dialectical relationship is captured with precision in the formula "constructing a landscape,"[58] used by Perrault in the project for a cultural center at Santiago de Compostela. This formula alludes literally to the architectural intervention, to the foundation of the project on the hill and the topographical changes that result as a consequence of the work of construction and elevation. In the figurative sense, however, the expression also refers to the fact that architecture and nature—"unspoiled" and "artificial"—are conceived as equal elements of the same topography.

The prism of rectangular glass, along with the site on which it stands, raises the center of the hill, emphasizing the crest by its own orientation and at the same time tracing the "natural" boundary between pinewood and meadow. In addition to the effect it produces as a volume in the landscape, the structure acquires full legibility only through its additional prerogatives as object, as "identifiable sign." It is only together with the architectural form that the top of the hill becomes what can be described as a "hill of culture"[59] and thus something more than a simple place that has been strongly emphasized. The hill and cultural center are comparable, in their unity, to the city with its cathedral and only the accent placed on the respective centers allows the two locations—the city and the hill—to be perceived, apart from their dimensions, as opposite poles: the city in the plain as a dense agglomerate with the cathedral at the center and the main square, the hill above as free elevation with its summit crowned: a dialectical relationship made fully evident by the mass of the cultural center. Thus the tops of the bell towers and the ridgeline of the glass prism are set at the same absolute height above sea level, the towers and the subterranean part of the prism, i.e. the usable zone, are at the same elevation, and the cathedral with the square in front has the same length as the prism. The comparison of the two buildings is made possible in the first place not by iconographic signs, but by formal characteristics that can be perceived by the senses. But the cultural center acquires full significance only with the precise choice of the object of comparison, the cathedral.

The similar disposition of masses and the use of the same material for the Hôtel Industriel and the prism of the cultural center, "an almost nothing and an I-don't-know-what" and a "hill of culture," show that, independently of their respective functions, the peculiarities of the form cannot be sufficient for a coherent architectural perception. Only the dual aspiration to an "identifiable sign" and an "unmistakable place" makes it possible to attain the necessary fusion of form and place: "This 'great moment,' this tangible meeting, is nothing but emotion."

"[…] and Protection of the Body"

"Some of these [first men] began […] to build huts roofed with branches, or dig caves in the mountains, or even to build shelters in which to take cover out of mud and sticks, imitating the technique used by swallows to construct their nests."[60] Legends of the origins of architecture have always proved useful means of looking beyond the forms that have been handed down. With his account of the invention of architecture, Vitruvius sought instead to get away from a presumed history of the origins and go back to the primitive forms of construction of the various peoples: hut, tent, cave, house, etc.

"Glass case" with "photo," "ladder" and "tree"[61]: these are the objects that characterize the layout devised by Perrault for the theme of the Kolonihavehus, housing for working-class neighborhoods in Denmark.[62] Four walls of glass, joined together to form an enclosed space, that circumscribe the place with geometric precision; a staircase linking the outside with the inside. Thus architecture is brought to a zero point, and reduced, as "projection of the mind and protection of the body," to its essential components: a transparent envelope of protection and the dematerialized appearance of a geometric form. Le Corbusier referred to the similar image of a regular hut with an enclosure to introduce one of his most complex arguments: the *"tracés régulateurs"* ("regulating layouts"): "It is the plan of a house, it is the plan of a temple. It is the same spirit as we find in the house of Pompeii. It is the spirit of the temple of Luxor. There are no primitive men, there are only primitive means. The idea is constant, *in posse* since the beginning."[63] The distinction between intellectual work and its material translation, between idea and architectural construction, allowed Le Corbusier not only to give his *"tracés régulateurs"* historical legitimacy, but also to set his buildings in the tradition of an architectural history regarded as basic and to compare them in terms that went beyond their formal aspect. When Perrault speaks of an enclosure for the Kolonihaven, a cave for the Villa Saint-Cast and an archetype for the seat of the Bibliothèque Nationale, the themes he is tackling are in essence the same as the ones discussed by Le Corbusier.

"This house, is it a house?"[64] The project for an underground villa at Saint-Cast raises the question of the fundamental form in which the house has found expression: "Can we rediscover the cave of humanity's early days as the original feeling of the presence of man on the earth?"[65] In

Dominique
Perrault,
Kolonihavehus
installation,
Copenhagen.

Dominique
Perrault, villa
at Saint-Cast.

legends of the origins as well, the cave is often indicated as one of the earliest forms of habitation. In its natural layout it constitutes a type of dwelling with less "architecture" than any other—at the most a wall—and therefore requires minimal manual skills. If someone were to postulate a return to the cave as an expression of the primeval dwelling and ask for a house "to live better with, in our environment,"[66] what he would be looking for would not at all be a romantic plunge into a primordial form of habitation, but a conception of the house as visible artifact in relationship with the surrounding landscape. Thus it is an act of imitation, not formal but conceptual, that identifies the task of architecture as confrontation with the environment. Living in nature does not mean living in contact with the earth, but reintegrating the house, conceived here as a masonry structure set on the ground, into the topographic context. It does not represent a means of protecting oneself from the natural environment, but a way of giving it an architectural configuration. Here lies the real difference between Vitruvius's cave, a natural phenomenon, and the house at Saint-Cast. The question raised prior to giving the house its configuration concerned not so much the form of dwelling as, in more concrete terms, the validity of the historical and typological conventions of architecture in its relationship with the environment. In his project for the Olympic facilities in Berlin, Perrault defined this as "a work on the absence of architecture in the academic sense of the term,"[67] and on another occasion as "escaping architecture"[68] and its stylistic rules, its inertia and the authority of its conventions.[69] By this he did not intend to condemn the discipline as a whole, but just an approach to it restricted to the historical and formal dimension. It is precisely in connection with the indoor swimming pool and the velodrome, cited by Perrault as examples of liberation from the problem of form, that we find an evocation of the historical model of the amphitheater.[70] "When something worth seeing is taking place on level ground and everybody crowds forward to look, those in the rear find various ways of raising themselves to see over the heads of those in front [...] By his [the architect's] art he creates as plain a crater as possible, and the public itself supplies its decoration."[71] In his lapidary assertion that a velodrome is circular and a swimming pool rectangular, Perrault takes these requirements into account. He is alluding to the form that results, not to the idea behind the design. "These amphitheaters hollowed out of the orchard [...] will be covered by two pieces of woven metal [...]."[72] What we have here is a crater with a velarium, a pit with a cover, two fundamental architectural elements[73]: the pit made of concrete, the cover a web of metal cables that run above a lattice structure. The independence of the two elements, separated from one another statically, is clearly visible. But only the formalization of the idea makes them truly perceptible and recognizable as a symbol, as a representation of their respective peculiarities, i.e. when the basin is filled with tiers of seating and the heavy roof gives the impression of a light material.

"Tables [...] covered with wire gauze"[74] or "nomad's tent, pitched there"[75]: these two textile

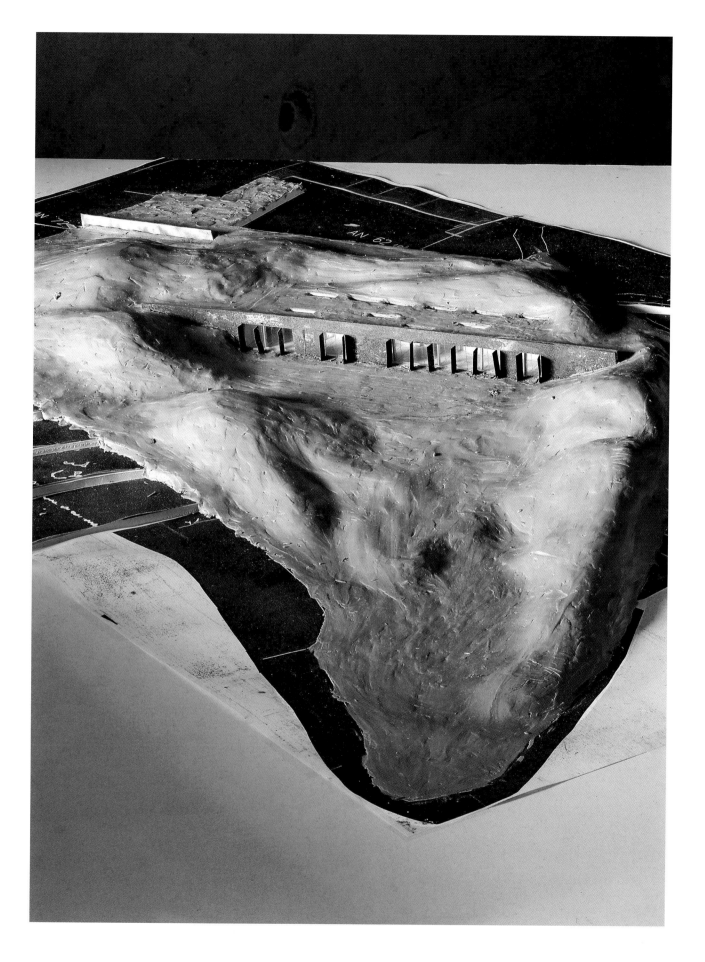

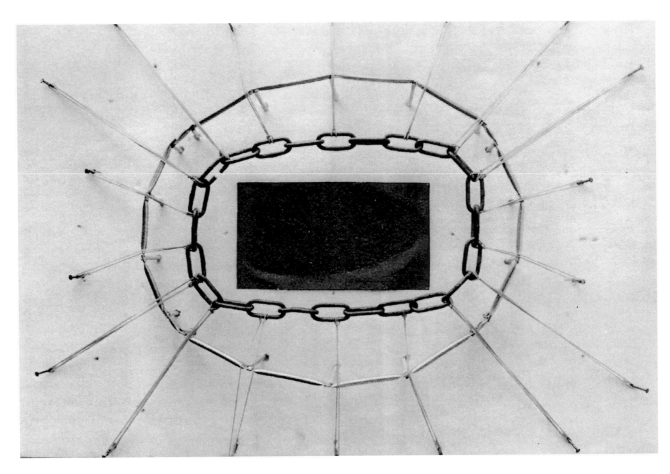

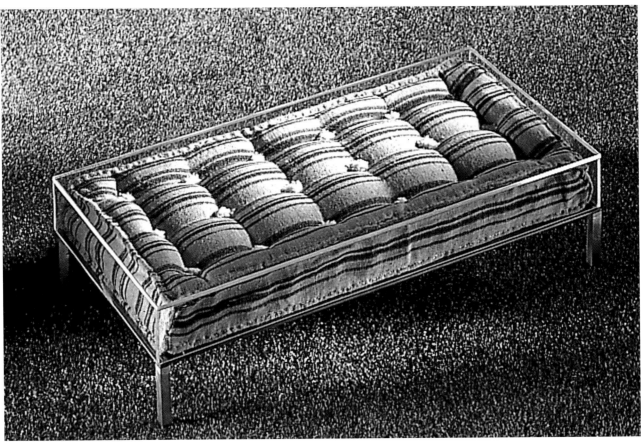

metaphors used for the Olympic facilities in Berlin and the football stadium at Badalona convey the different relationship with the two essential qualities of the material: that it hangs and that it is taut. If the metal cables were used in Berlin to cover the structure of the roof, at Badalona the physical properties of the metal web—its resistance to traction—govern the idea of the design from the technical and symbolic point of view. The ducts, connected to a central ring, are strung on pillars and anchored to the mountain and thus form an open roof above the football pitch. Here too the architectural form develops out of the dialogue between "concept" and "context," between idea of the tent and properties of the metal, out of exploration of the opposite requirements of form and matter. In essence, the individual design phases of the architectural process are conceived in the same way as the choices at the level of territory or place, of the layout of a square in Berlin or a new suburban landscape at Badalona.

When one parameter of the context—for instance the material, the function or the scale—is left out, the idea can in part acquire a conscious autonomy. These experiments make it possible to probe the limits between a valid idea and an unusable one and to study its associative character. In a dialectical sense, as addition of geometric structure and ergonomic function of seating, as framework and basin, the seat of the Bibliothèque de France integrates the two essential qualities of solidity and comfort. By contrast, in the bench-cum-bed of the WANAS-Foundation, which is made up of similar elements, of a glass framework on supports and a cushion as seat, the latter is incorporated into the structure itself. So if the two elements are present and visible, they are altered in their combination to such an extent that they no longer meet the needs of comfort. The WANAS-Foundation bench shows with ironic clarity that it is precisely the "characteristics of architecture forming utilitarian areas,"[76] avoided by Sol LeWitt since they would weaken the expressive force of art, that reinforce the architectural form, bestowing on it its essential meaning.

"Architecture: Projection of the Mind and Protection of the Body"

The idea of the death of architecture is not a new one. It is one of the recurrent themes of the discipline. Le Corbusier, who with his "And Vignola—at last—is done for! Thank you! Victory!"[77] looked forward to the death of codified architecture and who with his "theoretical observations," his "five points toward a new architecture," aimed to establish a "fundamentally new aesthetic"[78] but ended up giving rise to a new codification, has in the meantime been elevated, from the stylistic point of view at least, to the status of a classical type of modernity. But alongside the rejection and condemnation of academic traditions and the methods used to allow architecture to keep up with contemporary trends, the aspiration to the new has always been a search for the "reason for the existence of things,"[79] for the essence of architecture in its timelessness.

"The notion of process appears fully contemporary; it defines the idea of an accompaniment as well as that of an integration of procedures with a conceptual understanding of architecture."[80] Perrault outlines his conception of architectural activity without questioning the dichotomy between thought and material, without concealing the creative process that extends from the idea all the way to its material expression, but capturing it instead in all its different formulations. The inversion, simultaneity and superimposition of the means of representation—be they models, drawings, sketches, diagrams, etc.—that are discerned in the process of design, the reciprocal fertilizing action of "concept" and "process," the parallel road of the project and its realization, the use of the grid as a means not just of creating order, but also of generating openings and forms, the dialectical relationship between "unmistakable place" and "identifiable sign" and the link between archetype and random development are different aspects of a single method. So architecture is not regarded as a definitive result, but as a possible state within an unlimited process of development. Thus the aim of the project is not to fix a definitive form, but to create a figure for a specific period of time. This conception finds its clearest expression in the superimposition of the shaping "projection of the mind" on the contemplative "pure creation of the mind,"[81] but reaches its true fullness in the union of "architecture, projection of the mind and protection of the body."

1 Bernard Blistène and Xavier Douroux, "Un entretien entre Dominique Perrault et Claude Rutault," in *Claude Rutault chez Dominique Perrault*, ed. by the Centre national d'art et de culture Georges Pompidou / Centre d'art contemporain Dijon, Edips, Dijon 2000, p. 9.
2 *"Il est indispensable de quitter le champ traditionnel de l'architecture, de l'étendre à d'autres domaines, afin d'excéder le language constitué, de procéder par greffes, insémination artificielle."* Dominique Perrault, "Architecture effective," in *With Dominique Perrault*, Birkhäuser, Basel-Boston-Berlin 1999, p. 325.
3 Sol LeWitt, "Paragraphs on Conceptual Art," in Alexander Alberro and Blake Stimson, *Conceptual Art: a Critical Anthology*, MIT Press, Cambridge, Mass.-London 1999, p. 13 (*Artforum*, 5:10, 1967).
4 Ibid., p. 14.
5 *"Projection de l'esprit et protection du corps."* In Dominique Perrault and Gaëlle Lauriot-Prévost, "Concept – contexte. Exposition Galerie Denise Renée," in *Dominique Perrault*, Artemis, Zurich-Munich-London 1994, p. 105.
6 Marcus Vitruvius Pollio, *De architectura*. Translated from the Italian edition ed. by Giovanni Florian, Giardini, Pisa 1978, p. 8.
7 Leon Battista Alberti, *L'Architettura (De re aedificatoria)*, Latin text and Italian trans. ed. by G. Orlandi, intro. and notes by P. Portoghesi, I, Milan 1966, pp. 6–8.
8 *"Projection de l'esprit"* or *"l'idée,"* Dominique Perrault and Gaëlle Lauriot-Prévost, "Concept – contexte…", in op. cit., p. 105.
9 *"Incruster," "préserver," "inclure," "métisser."* Dominique Perrault, "Concepts," in Dominique Perrault, *Des natures. Au-delà de l'architecture*, ed. Architekturgallerie Luzern, Birkhäuser, Basel-Boston-Berlin 1996.
10 *"Notion d'opération"* or *"idée d'accompagnement."* Dominique Perrault, "Le temps du *process*," in *With Dominique Perrault*, cit. p. 144.
11 *"Le travail doit s'accomplir en simultané dans toutes les dimensions du* process *et il est nécessaire de recomposer pour chaque projet des outils, un language, des réponses plus adéquates."* Ibid., p. 143.
12 *"Une chaise + une chaise pour lire = une chaise de lecture"; "le château + le disque de verre = le double du château."*
13 *"Vision idéaliste du projet architectural."* Ibid. p. 144.
14 *"La séparation entre conception et réalisation s'estompe."* Ibid., p. 144.
15 *"Définir ce que pourrait être l'avenir."*
16 *"Premières propositions d'ambiance."*
17 *"Au fur et à mesure, s'inscrivant dans la durée, les programmes, aujourd'hui inconnus, viendrons prendre place."* Dominique Perrault, *Caen. Réaménagement du site de la SMN. Note de présentation*, October 1994.
18 *"Cette notion de process, d'opération."* Dominique Perrault, "Le temps du *process*," in op. cit., p. 145.
19 Dominique Perrault in conversation with the author, August 5, 2000.
20 *"Règles strictes de la géométrie et de la syntaxe d'une grille de mots croisés."* Dominique Perrault, *Aplix*, Lars Müller, Baden 1999.
21 *"Comme les lettres forment les mots."*
22 *"Principe esthétique produisant une forme architecturale non déterminée."*
23 Dominique Perrault, *Concorso internazionale di idee. L'industria della natura. Parco urbano aree Falck, Sesto San Giovanni*, presentation text for the competition, 1998.
24 Ibid.
25 Mel Bochner, "The Serial Attitude," in *Conceptual Art: a Critical Anthology*, cit., p. 22.
26 Sol LeWitt, op. cit., p. 15.
27 *"L'interrogation sur la capacité d'abstraction de l'architecture."* Dominique Perrault in conversation with the author, July 7, 2000.

28 *"[L'homme primitif] ne pouvait pas créer quelque chose autrement, qui lui donnât l'impression qu'il créait,"; "La géométrie est le language de l'homme."* Le Corbusier, *Vers une architecture*, Editions Arthaud, Paris 1977, p. 55.
29 Sol LeWitt, op. cit., p. 15.
30 *"Effets des corps."* Etienne-Louis Boullée, *Essai sur l'art*, preface by Jean-Marie Pérouse de Montclos, Hermann, Paris 1968, p. 35.
31 *"Emotion supérieure, d'ordre mathématique."* Le Corbusier, *Vers une architecture*, cit., p. 181.
32 *"Le 'less is more' de l'émotion."* Dominique Perrault, "Bibliothèque nationale de France," in *Dominique Perrault*, cit., p. 63.
33 *"Wie ist die Radsporthalle? Sie ist ein Kreis, die Schwimmsportshalle? Ein Rechteck. Punkt. Letztendlich finde ich, dass diese Feststellung – eine Radhalle ist rund, eine Schwimmhalle ist rechteckig – am besten zeigt, dass Architektur nicht in der Form steckt. Sie ist jenseits, ausserhalb."* Dominique Perrault, *Rad- und Schwimmsporthalle*, description of the project, 1999.
34 *"Corps simples en terme de géométrie."*
35 *"Les plus riches possible, les plus complexes, les plus variés, flexibles."* Dominique Perrault, "Les formes d'une unité," in *With Dominique Perrault*, cit., pp. 177–78.
36 Bernard Blistène and Xavier Douroux, "Un entretien entre Dominique Perrault et Claude Rutault…", in op. cit., p. 21.
37 Robert Morris, "Notes on Sculpture," in *Artforum*, vol. IV, n. 6, 1966, p. 44.
38 *"Le Parthénon apporte des certitudes: l'émotion supérieure, d'ordre mathématique. L'art, c'est la poésie."* Le Corbusier, *Vers une architecture*, cit., p. 181.
39 *"Les objets et leurs matières ne sont rien sans les lumières qui les transcendent."* Dominique Perrault, "Bibliothèque nationale de France," in *Dominique Perrault*, cit., p. 63.
40 Ibid., p. 62.
41 *"Nature immédiate et spécifique."* Dominique Perrault, "L'espace de l'émotion," in *With Dominique Perrault*, cit., p. 229.
42 *"L'intensité de la fonte."*
43 *"Cette espèce de force incroyable."*
44 *"Sicherlich sind die Formen ein Teil der Architektur, aber sie erklären sie nicht."* Dominique Perrault, *Rad- und Schwimmsporthalle*, cit., 1999.
45 *"Atteindre le cerveau sans passer par l'intellect."* Dominique Perrault, "L'espace de l'émotion," in op. cit., p. 228.
46 Carl Andre, catalogue of the exhibition at the Haags Gemeentemuseum, The Hague 1969, p. 5, quoted by David Bourdon, "A Redefinition of Sculpture," in *Carl Andre. Sculpture 1959–1977*, pub. by Laguna Gloria Art Museum, Austin 1978, p. 28.
47 *"Un-presque-rien-et-un-je-ne-sais-quoi."* Dominique Perrault, "Hôtel Industriel Jean-Baptiste Berlier," in *Dominique Perrault*, cit., p. 43.
48 *"Absence de l'architecture au sens académique du terme."* Dominique Perrault, "Vélodrome, Swimming Pool," in *Dominique Perrault*, cit., p. 72.
49 Dominique Perrault, "Recoudre, inscrire. Autoroute A 20, Brive-Montauban, France," in *Des natures…*, cit., p. 60.
50 Phyllis Tuchmann, "An interview with Carl Andre," in *Artforum*, June 1970, p. 55, quoted in David Bourdon, "A redefinition of sculpture…," in op. cit., p. 16.
51 *"En posant 'le château sur un plateau de verre,' on définit un lieu évident et un signe identifiable."* Dominique Perrault, "Centre de conférence Usinor-Sacilor," in *Dominique Perrault*, cit., p. 46.
52 *"Pourtant, tout ce processus de fabrication de l'édifice tient sur une rencontre, souvent fulgurante, entre un concept et un contexte, entre une idée et un lieu. Ce*

[52] "grand moment," ce rendez-vous sensible, n'est qu'émotion." Dominique Perrault and Gaëlle Lauriot-Prévost, "Concept – contexte…", in op. cit., p. 105.

[53] "Lorsque j'ai reçu le programme de 300.000 mètres carrés […] j'ai fait un volume de pâte à modeler simultanément à la maquette du site. J'ai posé mon volume en pâte à modeler et me suis dit que si je le réalisais comme tel, ce serait un véritable monstre, une masse opaque, un bunker." […] "Alors j'ai écrasé mon volume et n'ont subsisté que les quatres angles avec bien sûr les références multiples que je vous laisse deviner." Bernard Blistène and Xavier Douroux, "Un entretien entre Dominique Perrault et Claude Rutault," in op. cit., p. 21.

[54] "Point de départ d'une restructuration totale de toute cette partie du 13ème arrondissement"; "un lieu qui s'inscrit dans la continuité de la succession des grands vides accrochés à la Seine, tels la Place de la Concorde, le Champs de Mars, les Invalides." Dominique Perrault, Une place pour Paris. Une Bibliothèque pour la France, Institut Français d'Architecture, Paris 1989, p. 41.

[55] "Il est toutefois nécessaire de prendre en compte l'histoire, mais comme une donnée parmi les autres, et ce qui est déterminant dans cette histoire, c'est qu'elle a produit une géographie d'un certain type." Dominique Perrault, "L'architecte dans son contexte," in With Dominique Perrault, cit., p. 59.

[56] "Une place pour Paris, une Bibliothèque pour la France." Dominique Perrault, Une place pour Paris…, cit., p. 3.

[57] "On ne présumera pas que l'auteur de ce projet, en décrivant la sublime image que présentera le lieu dont il est question, ait eu le dessein de parler de l'art qu'il pourra employer pour la décoration de ce monument. Il assure qu'elle proviendrait de son immensité." Etienne-Louis Boullée, op. cit., p. 131.

[58] "Construire un paysage." Dominique Perrault, Cidade da Cultura de Galicia, presentation text for the competition, 1999.

[59] "Colline de la culture."

[60] Marcus Vitruvius Pollio, op. cit., p. 32.

[61] "Etui de verre"; "photo"; "échelle"; "arbre."

[62] Kolonihaven. The International Challenge, ed. by Arken Museum of Modern Art, Rhodos International, Copenhagen 1996.

[63] "C'est le plan d'une maison, c'est le plan d'un temple. C'est le même esprit que l'on retrouve dans la maison de Pompéi. C'est l'esprit du temple de Louqsor. Il n'y a pas d'homme primitif; il y a des moyens primitifs. L'idée est constante, en puissance dès le début." Le Corbusier, Vers une architecture, cit., p. 53.

[64] "Cette maison, est-elle une maison?" Dominique Perrault, "Villa Saint-Cast," in With Dominique Perrault, cit., p. 197.

[65] "Peut-on retrouver la grotte des premiers jours de l'humanité comme sentiment originel de la présence de l'homme sur la terre?" Ibid.

[66] "De mieux vivre avec, dans notre environnement."

[67] "Un travail sur l'absence de l'architecture au sens académique du terme." Dominique Perrault, "Vélodrome, Swimming Pool," in Dominique Perrault, cit., p. 72.

[68] "Echapper à l'architecture." Dominique Perrault in conversation with the author, July 7, 2000.

[69] Ibid.

[70] Dominique Perrault, "Vélodrome, Swimming Pool," in Dominique Perrault, cit., p. 72.

[71] "Wenn etwas Schauwürdiges auf flacher Erde vorgeht und alles zuläuft, suchen die Hintersten auf alle möglichen Weise sich über die Vordersten zu erheben […] Er [der Architekt] bereitet einen solchen Krater durch Kunst, so einfach als nur möglich, damit dessen Zierat das Volk selbst werde." Johann Wolfgang von Goethe, Italienische Reise, Könemann, Cologne 1998, p. 41. English trans. in Johann Wolfgang von Goethe, Italian Journey, Penguin, Harmondsworth 1970, p. 52.

[72] "Ces amphithéâtres creusés dans le verger […] seront abrités par deux pièces de metal tissé […]."

[73] Cf. Gottfried Semper, Die vier Elemente der Baukunst, Friedrich Vieweg und Sohn, Braunschweig 1851, p. 55.

[74] "Tables […] nappées d'un tissu métallique" Dominique Perrault, "Vélodrome et piscine olympiques," in With Dominique Perrault, cit., p. 329.

[75] "Tente de nomade, posée là" Dominique Perrault, Ajuntament de Badalona – Stade de Montigala et abords, description of the project, May 1998.

[76] Sol LeWitt, "Paragraphs on Conceptual Art," in op. cit., p. 15.

[77] "Et Vignole – enfin – est foutu! Merci! Victoire!" Le Corbusier, Le poème de l'angle droit, Editions Verve, Paris 1955, p. 68.

[78] "Theoretische Betrachtung en"; "Fünf Punkte zu einer neuen Architektur"; "fundamental neue fsthetik." Le Corbusier and Pierre Jeanneret, "Fünf Punkte zu einer neuen Architektur," in Bau und Wohnung, ed. by the Deutscher Werkbund, Akad. Verlag Dr. F. Wedekind & Co., Stuttgart 1927, p. 27.

[79] "Raison d'être des choses." Le Corbusier, Précisions sur un état présent de l'architecture et de l'urbanisme, Editions Vincent, Fréal & Cie., Paris 1960, p. 34.

[80] "La notion de process apparaît comme pleinement contemporaine, elle définit l'idée d'un accompagnement mais aussi celle d'une intégration des procédures à une compréhension conceptuelle de l'architecture." Dominique Perrault, "Le temps du process," in op. cit., p. 144.

[81] "Pure création de l'esprit." Le Corbusier, Vers une architecture, cit., pp. 159 ff.

Works and Projects

Hôtel Industriel Jean-Baptiste Berlier
Paris, 1986–90

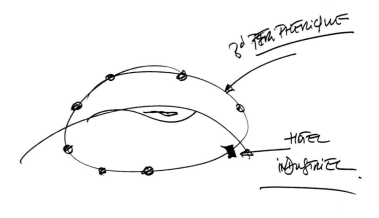

In 1986 the Municipality of Paris held a competition for the utilization of a plot of land in the 13th arrondissement, located between a slip road leading to the Quai d'Ivry and the railroad lines of the Gare d'Austerlitz. The competition announcement spoke of a *hôtel industriel*, a term that signifies neither an office block nor a building to be used exclusively for production, but a flexible space that is able to house a multiplicity of light industrial activities on a medium scale that take up a limited amount of space.

The context in which the building is set represents a fragment of the contemporary city characterized by warehouses, industrial sheds, concrete silos, a helicopter-rescue pad and a center for the control and regulation of fast traffic. The Berlier complex—which among other things houses the Perrault studio —stands out from it like a crystalline prism, an example of one of those eye-catching buildings that characterize the new look of the eastern zone of Paris.

The construction is able to house 17,000 square metres of manufacturing activities of various dimensions distributed on ten levels, corresponding to some forty companies and 500 employees: figures that are bound to change constantly over time along with the organization and internal arrangement of the building, characterized by the maximum of flexibility. In fact, unlike numerous examples of buildings used for the same purpose, it does not present itself as an architectural object in its own right, but is perceived by means of the activities that go on inside it, in virtue of its transparence.

Designed to give the impression of a block of glass, it is supported by structural elements located behind the transparent surface. Their visibility creates an immediate sense of depth. Panes of glass adhering to the structure cover the whole of the building. The absence of visible pillars permits the sky and its reflected image to encounter one another. The 1148 panels are fixed on tracks that were installed at the time the concrete part was poured and connected to the beams so that the force of the wind is transmitted to the entire structure. Given the high level of noise in the area, the glass panels cannot be opened. A proportion of them have been made thinner, so that they can be broken in case of fire. In 1992 the design received the Constructa Preis, a European award for industrial architecture, and in 1990 it was given the Prix Amo, Architecture et maître d'ouvrage.

Study sketch of the location.

Profile of the building in its context.

Nighttime view.

*Study sketch
of the materials
and the lighting.*

Daytime view.

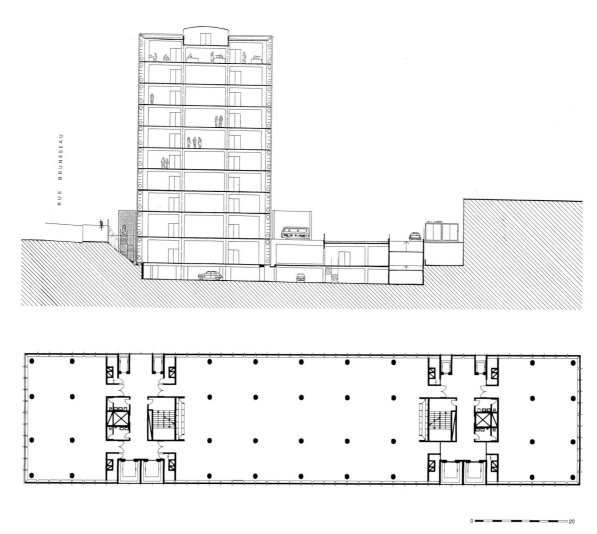

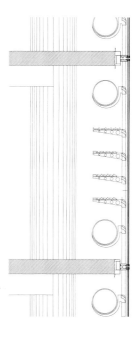

View of the structural elements located behind the glazed surface.

Structural detail of the façade.

31

IRSID, Usinor-Sacilor Convention Center
Saint-Germain-en-Laye, 1989–91

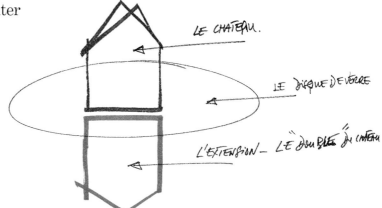

The competition announcement for this convention center, to be housed in the nineteenth-century Château de Saint-Léger at Saint-Germain-en-Laye, required an auditorium with two hundred seats and twelve meeting rooms. The winning project was guided by the decision not to annex a new structure to the existing building, something that would have altered its character irremediably, but to enhance it by setting it on a transparent disk. It is underneath this, embedded in the ground, that the more "public" spaces (the auditorium, restaurant and cafeteria; the old building has been used for the meeting rooms) have been located, while on the outside it functions as a catalyzing element on which the access routes converge.

In the daytime the disk of glass and steel filters the natural light and reflects the silhouette of the castle and the park that surrounds it, as if in a pool of water. At night it illuminates them spectacularly from below. Constructed with a double facing that is accessible for inspection and fitted with adjustable panels, it also performs the function of a filter to control the temperature and the quality of the air.

A metal footbridge spans the reflective surface and leads to the castle. At the center of the latter access is provided to the spaces underground. These are arranged concentrically: in the middle, and therefore directly beneath the castle, the zone of circulation, then the spaces of the restaurant and auditorium and finally a technical "belt," housing the service entrances and emergency exits.

Study sketch and side view of the castle.

32

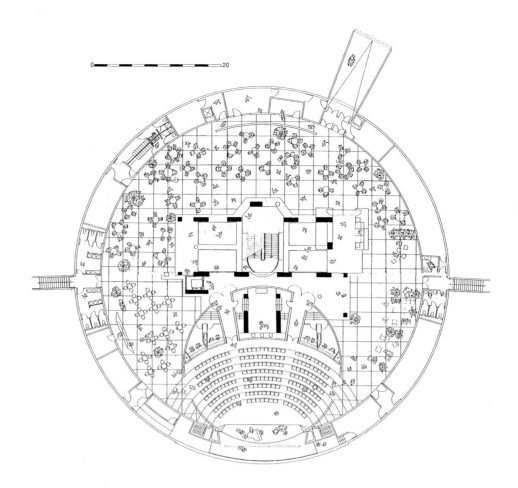

Plan of the auditorium at the level of the garden; view of the front with the footbridge of access.

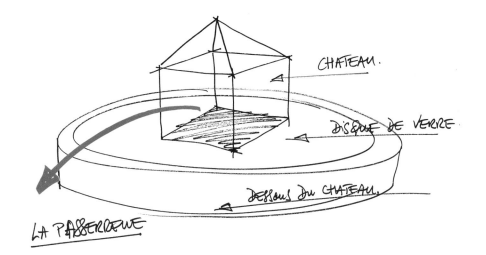

CHATEAU.

DISQUE DE VERRE.

DESSOUS DU CHATEAU.

LA PASSERELLE

Sketch of the elements of the project, views of the footbridge at the entrance.

34

Details of the glass roof of the auditorium area from the outside and inside, sectioned model of the complex, structural detail of the glazing.

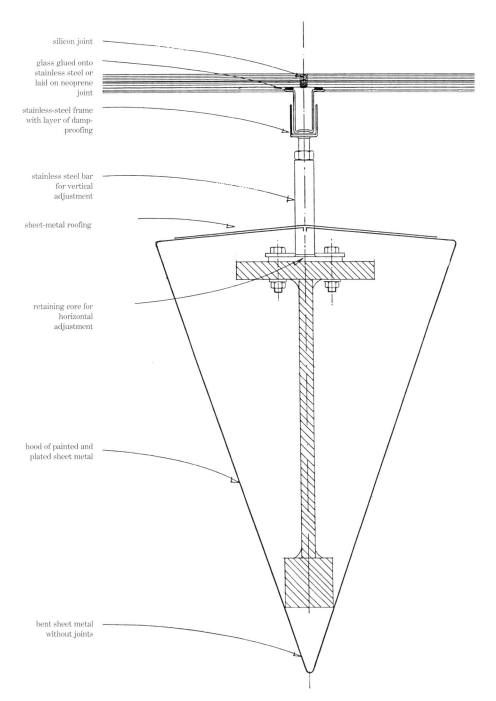

silicon joint

glass glued onto stainless steel or laid on neoprene joint

stainless-steel frame with layer of damp-proofing

stainless steel bar for vertical adjustment

sheet-metal roofing

retaining core for horizontal adjustment

hood of painted and plated sheet metal

bent sheet metal without joints

Bibliothèque Nationale de France
Paris, 1989–95

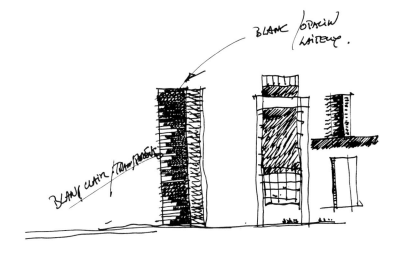

The design of the library (which had to be capable of housing twenty million volumes on four hundred kilometers of shelving, as well as facilities for four thousand readers) was guided by the desire to create a "place," a space, rather than a building in the proper sense of the word: located on an industrial site in the 13th arrondissement, on the banks of the Seine, the space echoes the other great "voids" in the Parisian urban continuum—Place de la Concorde, the Champ de Mars, the Invalides.

This intention has resulted in a minimalist work of architecture, totally devoid of ostentation, an urban "gesture" that is open horizontally and identified solely by the verticality of the towers that delimit it. The latter are shaped like open books and embody the metaphor of the accumulation of knowledge, while the square-cum-garden that they enclose recalls the peace and quiet of medieval cloisters. Light plays a fundamental role in the design: by day it penetrates and spreads through the transparent volumes; the artificial lighting forms a halo around the square and, by night, transforms the towers into luminous beacons.

Access to the library is provided by the great ramp facing onto the Seine, which then crosses the large square on the roof and descends into the green heart of the garden: a sort of journey of initiation into knowledge. Around the garden are arranged the thematic libraries (current affairs, sound/image, study, research), set on mezzanines that punctuate a 12-meter-high volume.

Completely open to the vegetation in the courtyard, these reading spaces are of variable geometry and therefore absolutely flexible. They are served along the perimeter by a system of facilities providing readers with the most advanced technological support.

The materials chosen for the facings and furnishings are wood and metal, with the aim of creating an atmosphere that is at once warm and austere, underlined by the almost intimate scale generated by the serried sequence of corridors and bookshelves. Silence and seclusion, necessary to study, are guaranteed by the disposition of the spaces of circulation, which in a manner of speaking "turn their backs" on the reading rooms. A similar function is performed by the technical blocks, whose height and thickness produce a sort of impermeability with respect to the zones of passage. The books requested by readers are delivered from the towers, which also house the administrative services.

Study sketch for the facing of the towers, views from the Seine and the embankment.

opposite
General view.

36

View onto
the internal
garden.

Plan at the level
of the covering of
the embankment.

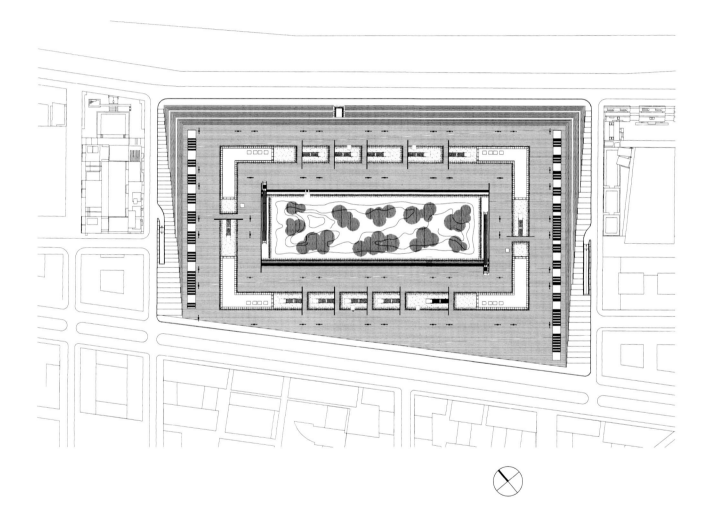

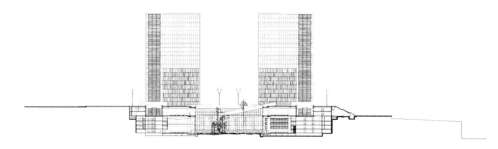

*Cross section, view
of the access zone.*

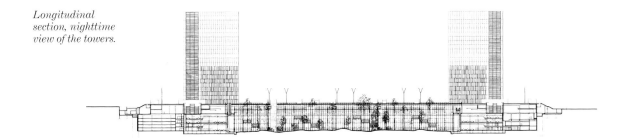

Longitudinal section, nighttime view of the towers.

*View from the
internal garden;
plan at the level
of the entrance,
information desk
and public reading
rooms, height
+35.20, with
furnishings, and
plan at the level of
the garden, height
+20.50, with
reading and
research rooms,
without
furnishings.*

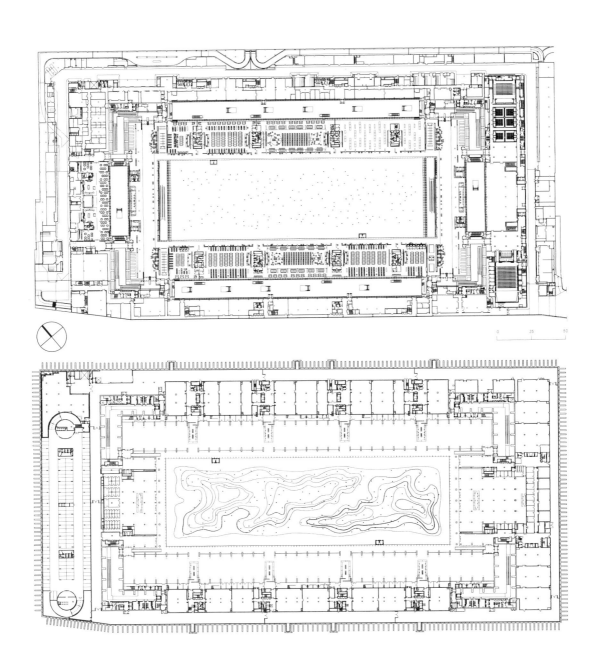

*Study sketches
of the connections,
views of the
circulation spaces.*

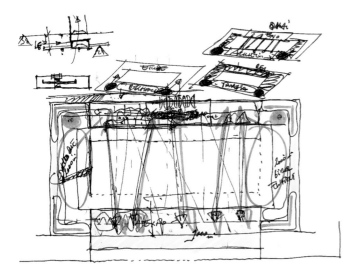

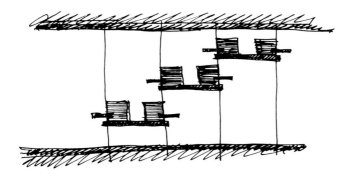

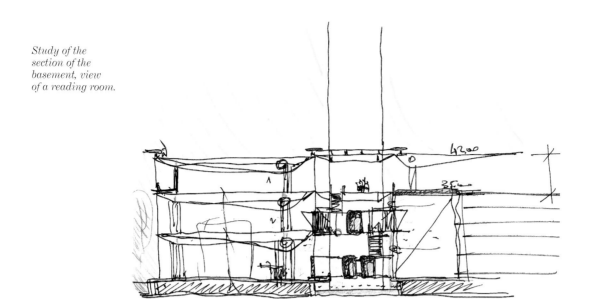

*Study of the
section of the
basement, view
of a reading room.*

Olympic Velodrome and Swimming Pool
Berlin, 1992–99

BERLIN

Les POMMIERS

LE SOL NATUREL

DESSUS

DESSOUS

The project, winner of the competition held at the time of Berlin's bid to hold the Olympic games in 2000, falls within the overall plan for the reunification of the two Germanies and the redevelopment of an entire zone of the German capital.

The area chosen is located at the intersection of two important axes of the city—a major axis that runs from the Alexanderplatz in the direction of Moscow and a minor one formed by a railroad line—and of two types of urban fabric. The problematic character of the intersection of the two systems militated against the insertion of further, confusing architectural features, which would have created an effect of additional disunity. Therefore, the decision was taken to make the two large building-containers (the circular one of the velodrome, for 9000 spectators, and the rectangular one of the swimming pool,

with a capacity of 4000) "vanish," creating at the same time a large open-air public space, a park planted with apple trees in which sports facilities have also been located. They are almost totally "sunk" into the ground, with only their roofs of metal and glass emerging. In the daytime they resemble pools of water, at night they create a particularly suggestive illumination.

The park created is an "orchard" with "wild" cider apples imported from Nor-

mandy and arranged at random. To encourage the population of the park with fauna it is suggested that other species of plant typical of the spontaneous vegetation to be found on railroad embankments be introduced.

To complete the upgrading of the district a series of highrise constructions is planned around the square: hotels, housing, offices and stores that can be varied to meet the requirements of local development.

Study sketch, aerial view of the location.

*Longitudinal
section of the
complex, view
of the velodrome
roof.*

following pages
*General view
of the exterior
of the complex.*

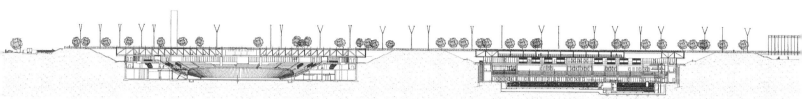

*Partial views
of the exterior.*

*Detail of the
velodrome roof,
plan of the complex
at the level of the
garden, the access
to the velodrome.*

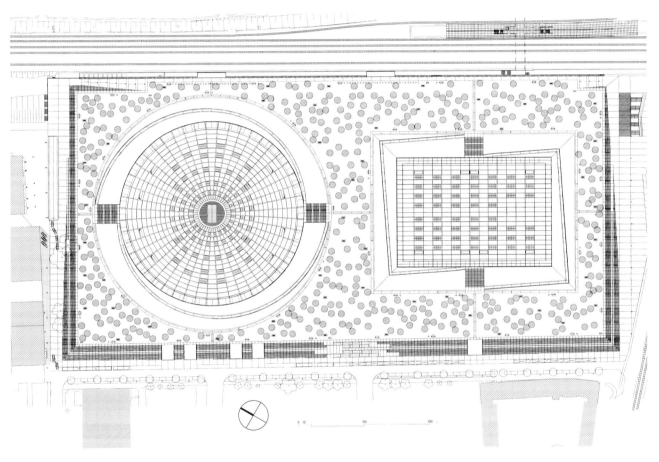

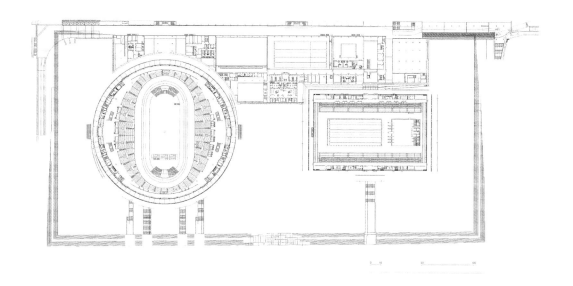

*Plan at the level
of the gallery and
the entrances for
the public, view
of the velodrome.*

*The diving area
and a swimming
pool.*

Centre Technique du Livre
Bussy Saint-Georges, 1993–95

The building was commissioned by the French Ministry of Public Education and the Bibliothèque Nationale de France. On a total area of over 65,000 square meters it houses the deposits for documents, newspapers and periodicals and for audiovisuals of scientific interest, as well as the facilities for repair and conservation of documents and books. In fact the specimens stored there are archive copies that are rarely consulted, such as graduate theses. Taking into account the infrequency with which it will be necessary to move them, a system of industrial storage has been adopted, with shelving reaching a height of ten meters.

The workshops are subdivided on the basis of their function, distinguishing the different treatments to which documents and books are subjected: reproduction on microfilm, deacidification and strengthening of the paper, treatment of audiovisuals.

Alongside these activities, a technical and scientific laboratory carries out research into conservation techniques and the quality control of standard processes and the biological and climatic characteristics of the deposits.

*Views of
the complex.*

*Elevations
and sections,
exterior view.*

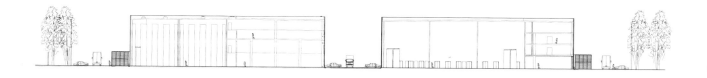

Details of the exteriors.

*Plans of the
ground floor; views
of the storage
shelving.*

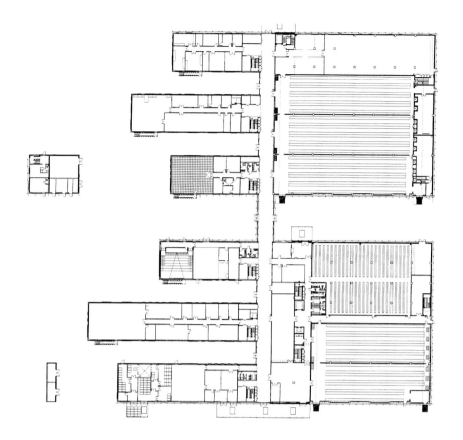

La Grande Serre, La Villette
Paris, 1996–98

Located in the Cité des Sciences et de l'Industrie at La Villette, the conservatory houses a permanent exhibition on new systems of cultivation. The total area of 800 square meters is laid out on two levels, used respectively for information and consultation services—the space of communication—and the greenhouse proper—the experimental space.

It was necessary to ensure a certain continuity in the movement of visitors through the Cité, and therefore to avoid erecting visual or material barriers that would cut the conservatory off from the other expositions. At the same time, however, there was a desire to create a protected place, a sort of mysterious "world apart." So the space of communication is completely open and defined only by slender metal pillars. The greenhouse proper, on the upper level, is entirely surrounded by a semitransparent fabric like the kind used in horticulture, which also has the function of characterizing and emphasizing the presence of the exhibition space, whose visual impact is amplified by the light it gives off.

The first space that visitors enter is absolutely flexible and can change over the course of time, through the updating and renewal of the installations. Then they climb to the upper level where they can interact with a true living laboratory.

The whole volume is overhung by a grill, suspended from the structure of the Cité, to which the covering fabric is attached and in which are set the remote lighting fixtures, which allow the plants to grow without raising the temperature inside the greenhouse to too high a level.

Detail with the protective awning lowered, study sketch.

opposite
View through the interior.

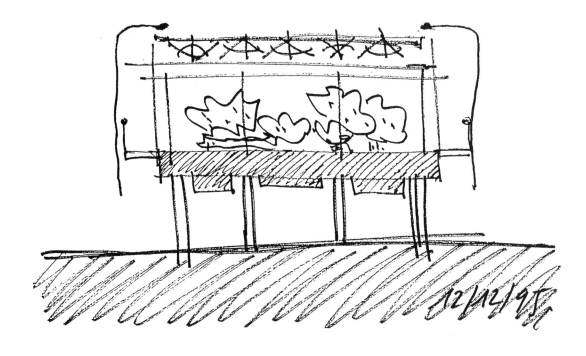

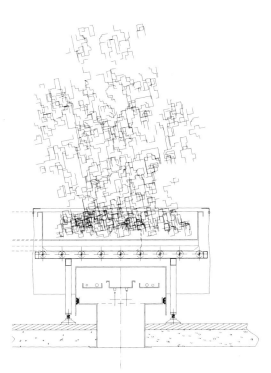

Cultivation tanks, cross section of a standard cultivation tank.

61

Plan of Reclamation of the Unimetal Area
Caen, 1995–97

On the outskirts of Caen, bounded by the bank of the river Orne and the built-up areas of Colombelles and Le Plateau, lies the area once occupied by the Société Métallurgique de Normandie. The subject of the competition was the reutilization of its northeast portion and the redefinition of the transport system.

From an examination of the territory it seemed clear that the disappearance of this important center of production and its unmistakable silhouette has left a gap, creating an imbalance in the landscape. Equally, the cessation of use of the transport system (road, rail and river) that served the industry has affected an area much larger than that of the site proper. Thus its reorganization and up-grading are of importance to the entire region of Caen.

The planning has been guided by the intention of carrying out a thorough study of what already exists so that it can be re-utilized. No grand development scheme, therefore, nor any new built-up areas with no links with the history of the territory, but a system capable of restoring significance to the traces already present in the natural landscape and the one shaped by human forces.

The elements revealed by the analysis of the landscape to be the points from which to set about reinforcing this tie were the course of the Orne, along which a tree-lined avenue would link the new and old residential area to Caen; the layout of a route that cut through the industrial installations transversally; and the disposition of the installations, seen as a prefiguration of the guidelines for urbanization. The backbone of the whole system is the ridgeline formed by the border between valley and plain.

So the plan of urbanization provides first of all an orientation, while the building proposals are susceptible to modification over the course of time, to meet new needs as they arise. A number of starting points were already provided by the decision to preserve a few constructions symbolic of the abandoned industry, such as the cooling tower that becomes the emblem of the new district and evokes the activity of the past.

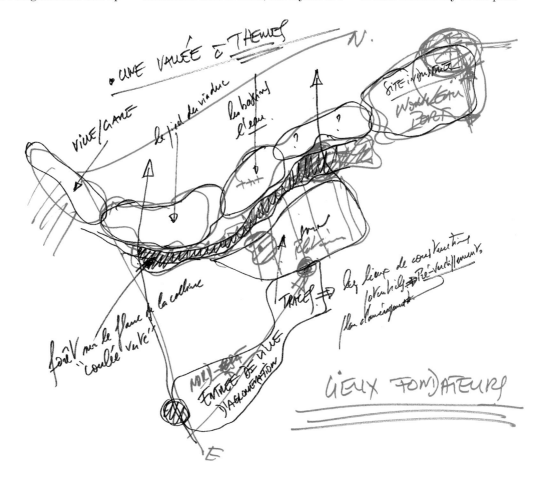

Sketch summarizing the generative elements of the plan.

*Proposal for
organization
of the site,
structural grid.*

Details of the first interventions in the landscape.

67

Enlargement of the Court of Justice of the European Union
Luxembourg, 1996–2007

The competition program required 10,500 square meters of offices and other premises for the presidency, members of the court and the chancellery, audience chambers, a library, a restaurant and parking facilities.

Fruit of a careful urbanistic analysis that led to the identification of a large square—the main courtyard—as the hub around which to structure all the functions of the complex, the proposal, which won the competition, is divided into distinct phases of operation that correspond to four distinct but correlated architectural elements. The first consists of the existing building, which will be completely gutted and stripped of the asbestos present, but whose metal structure and façades, fitted with sunscreens, will be retained. Inside it will be located new audience chambers and spaces of circulation, including elevators and escalators. All round this "historic" core runs the structure intended to house the offices, supported by slender columns to form a sort of peristyle. The third element is the gallery that connects and distributes the different areas of the complex, onto which open the existing audience chambers. The cafeteria, restaurant, library and other services are also arranged along the gallery in the form of kiosks. A genuine urban passage, which is matched underground by a route reserved for service vehicles, is covered by panes of glass through which it receives overhead light. Two towers for offices, located right next to the main courtyard, will complete the intervention and signal the presence of the Court in the urban panorama.

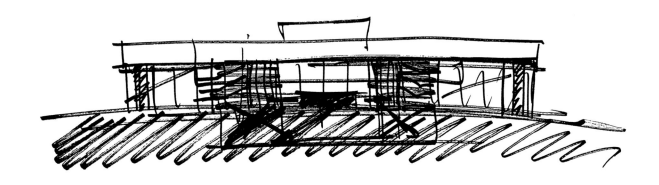

Study sketch for the enlargement of the existing building, model of the project in January 1998.

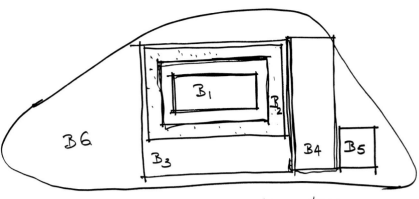

B1 = PALAIS.
B2 = ANNEAU.
B3 = SOCLE.
B4 = TOUR 1
B5 = TOUR 2

B6 = Aménagements EXT. /PAYSAGE

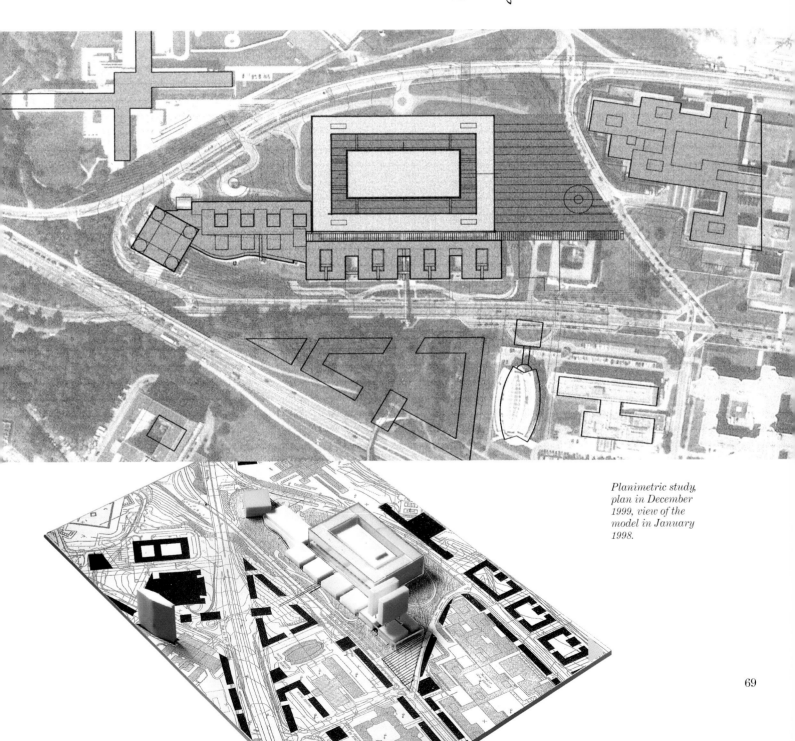

*Planimetric study,
plan in December
1999, view of the
model in January
1998.*

69

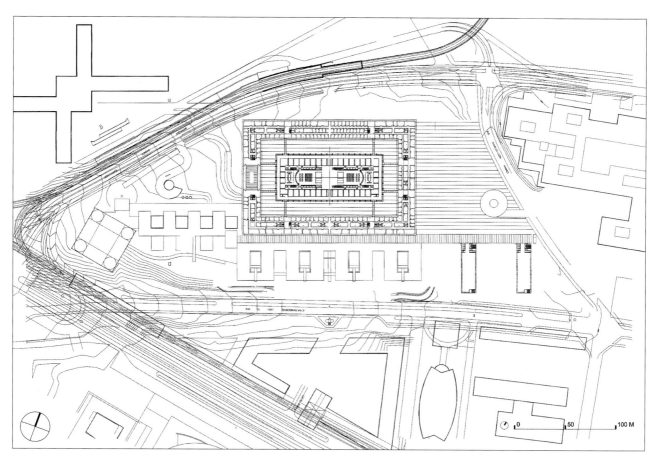

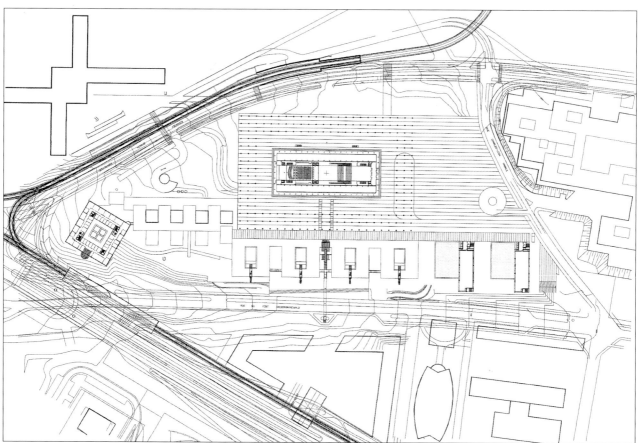

opposite
*Plans at levels 6
and 7 and at level
3, December 1999.*

*Views of the model
in December 1998,
cross section in
December 1998.*

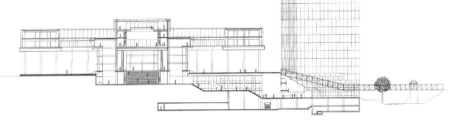

71

Aplix Factory
Le-Cellier-sur-Loire, 1997–99

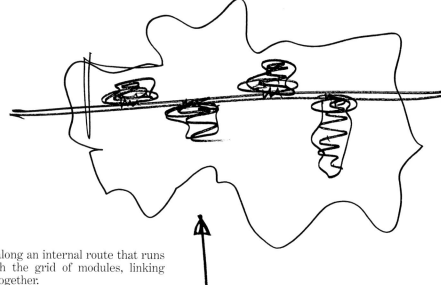

The use of a construction for industrial purposes means that the architecture has to be able to adapt very rapidly to changes in the production process. This entails an extreme application of the concept of flexibility, something that all too often leads to architecturally nondescript and banal forms.

For the Aplix plant and offices an attempt has been made to marry functionality with a simple but recognizable architectural vocabulary.

The buildings are arranged according to the geometric and syntactic rules of the crossword: each square in the grid, measuring 20 meters on a side, houses one function or part of a function; the functions interlock and intersect with one another in turn according to the progress of the manufacturing process. The company's entire activity is organized along an internal route that runs through the grid of modules, linking them together.

Shiny metal scales have been chosen for the facings that function as an optical device (Fresnel lens), multiplying or reducing the rays of light: the surrounding fields and woods are reflected in them with a strong impact on the landscape that, paradoxically, enhances the natural context by "dissolving" the constructed part. The pattern of reflections also performs a distorting action, as it makes it impossible to precisely gauge the scale of the buildings, to grasp their actual dimensions. Vegetation plays an important role inside the industrial area as well, in the form of large flower beds and gardens around which—like the words around the black boxes—the life of the factory unfolds.

Study sketch of the installation, planimetric scheme.

Views of the complex in the landscape.

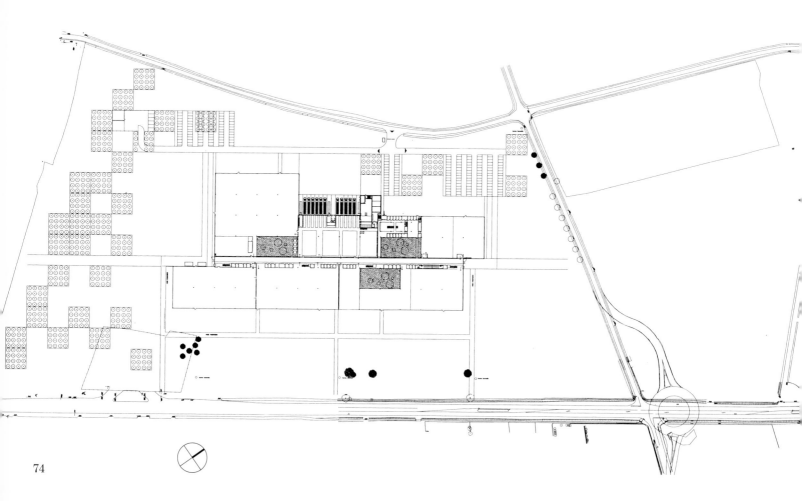

74

*Details of the
reflective facing,
general plan,
partial
longitudinal
sections.*

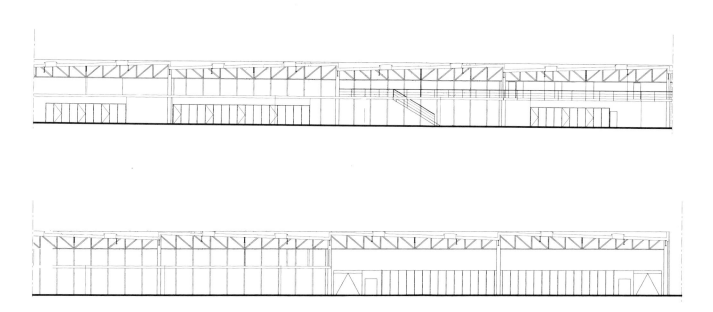

Mediathèque
Vénissieux, 1997–2001

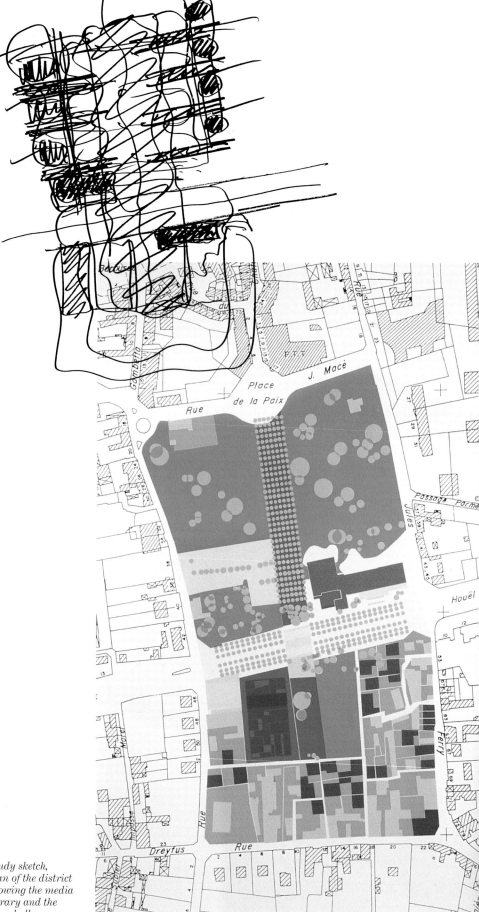

The site chosen for the construction of the Mediathèque was characterized by a low density of construction and a strong presence of vegetation, which had to be preserved and made the most of. The first step entailed the transformation of the urban axis that cuts the district in two into a grand tree-lined avenue; onto it face the two areas of greenery that surround the city hall and the media library. The intersection between this avenue and the north-south axis that runs alongside the city hall gives rise to a cross-shaped system on the basis of which the two blocks are geometrically and functionally organized, and a link is created between the historic center and the southern part of the city. The urbanization comprises a variety of elements and proceeds more by the addition of fragments than by following an abstract program: along a dense network of lanes are set more green areas, parking lots and houses with gardens, in which the emphasis is placed on the scale already present in this part of the city.

The media library, conceived as a multifunctional space open onto the city where is it possible to encounter and mix together different cultures, sensibilities and generations, looks like a glass box. Inside it the functions are located on a single level, surrounded by a gallery that allows visitors to walk around the entire perimeter of the building as well as performing a function of thermal and acoustic insulation from the outside. The Mediathèque is then cut transversally by a hall, a sort of urban passage between the square, to the west, and the lawn, east. From here access is provided to the offices, situated in a higher part of the building. They constitute an independent section, but one that is still linked to the activities of the media library, and are reminiscent of those transparent objects whose internal mechanism is left visible. The surfaces used for filling are colored and consist of simple and economical materials: in addition to glass, there is raw concrete, cement for the flooring and structures in galvanized steel.

Study sketch, plan of the district showing the media library and the town hall.

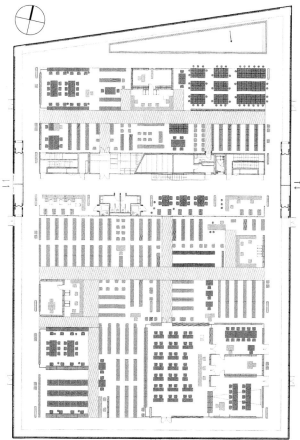

*Model of the
district, plan
of the new building,
study model.*

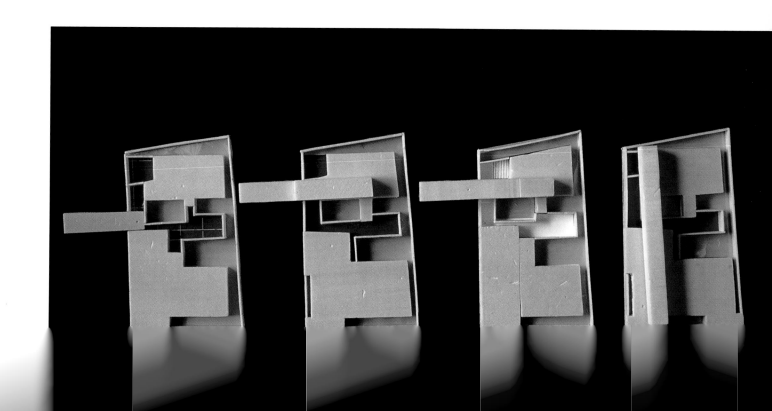

*Nighttime view,
study sketch, west
façade.*

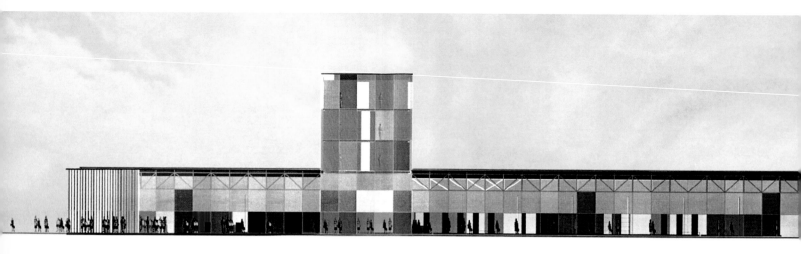

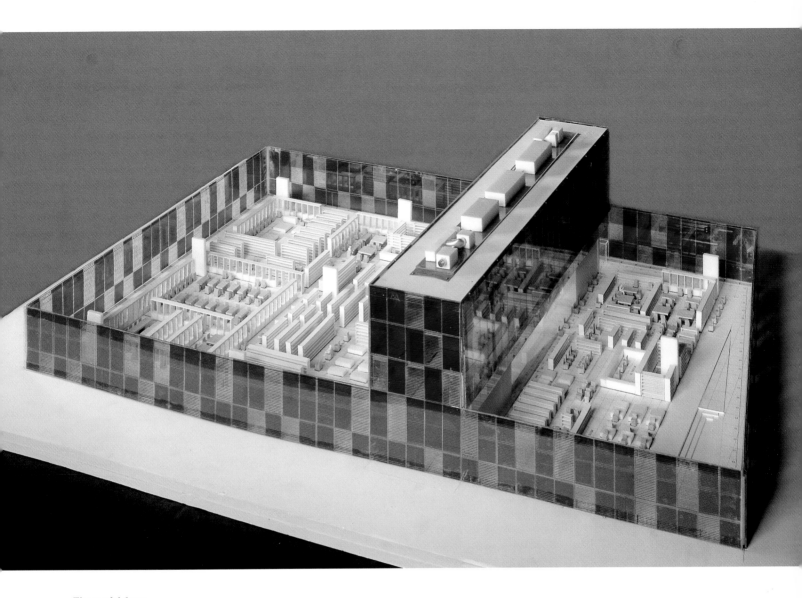

The model from
above, longitudinal
section.

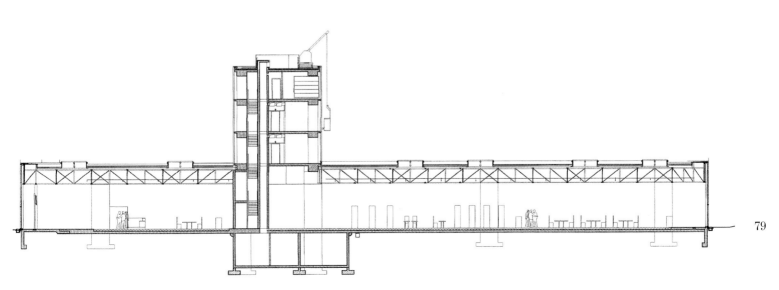

Urban Development Scheme and Sports Facilities
Badalona, 1998–2002

The valley of Batlloria, on the outskirts of Badalona, has been chosen for the construction of a sports complex comprising a stadium with a capacity of 8000, training facilities and a sports center with swimming pools, basketball pitches and gymnasiums. The undertaking includes the urbanistic reorganization and landscaping of the entire area, seen as a zone of services dedicated to sporting and recreational activities and an opportunity to harmonize nature and architecture.

To achieve this objective it was necessary to preserve as much as possible of the geography of the site, avoiding the introduction of "incongruous" architectural objects. Thus the structure with the greatest impact, the stadium, has been set inside a sort of crater, following the topographical conformation of the site. The only part of it visible is the protective covering, a mesh of woven metal that recalls the tent of a nomad encampment.

On the other hand, this new district devoted to sport and open-air activities has to establish a relationship with the rest of the town. To this end the disposition of the installations follows a sequence that runs from a more markedly urban and dense zone, where the facilities for local use are located, to the more rarefied and naturalistically interesting part constituted by the park, in the direction of the mountain. Within the sequence, all the spaces appear to be linked together like a "network" of interconnected services.

The starting point for defining the organization of the routes within the area was the topographical position of the valley itself, between the sea and the mountain and bounded by two expressways: thus a route has been laid out from the "lower" expressway (lower city) to the "upper" expressway (upper city) that takes on different forms according to the context: an urban and tree-lined avenue in the zone of high density, a path or lane when it crosses the park.

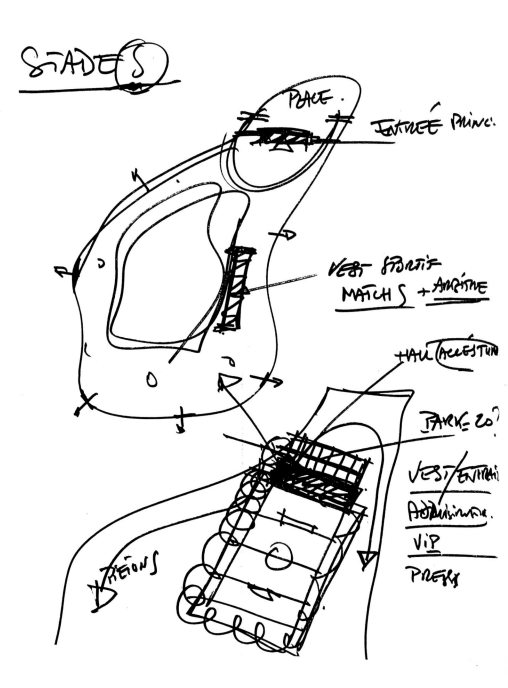

*Sketches of the
urbanization
scheme and the
sports complex.*

*Views of the model
of the complex,
axonometric
projection
of the stadium.*

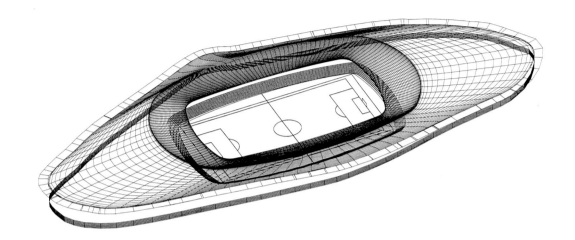

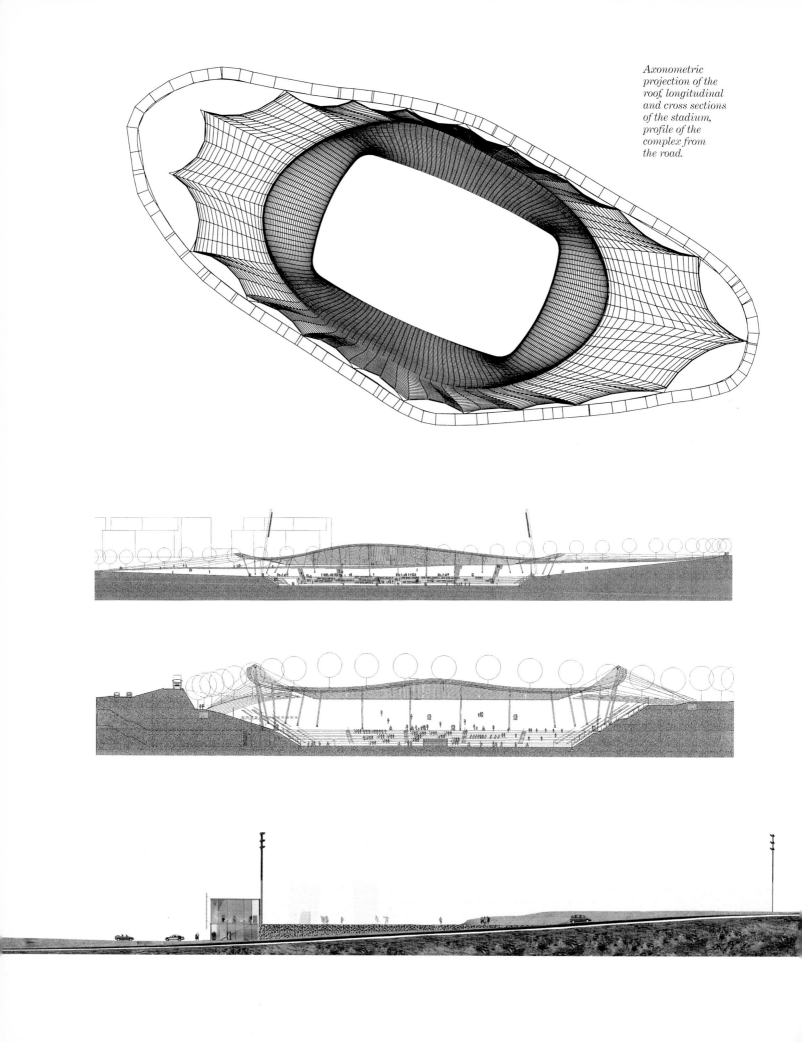

Axonometric projection of the roof, longitudinal and cross sections of the stadium, profile of the complex from the road.

*View of the model,
studies of shading.*

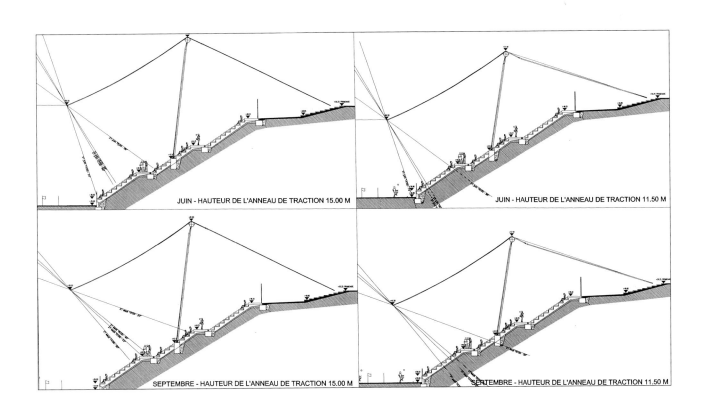

JUIN - HAUTEUR DE L'ANNEAU DE TRACTION 15.00 M

JUIN - HAUTEUR DE L'ANNEAU DE TRACTION 11.50 M

SEPTEMBRE - HAUTEUR DE L'ANNEAU DE TRACTION 15.00 M

SEPTEMBRE - HAUTEUR DE L'ANNEAU DE TRACTION 11.50 M

Landscaping Project
for the Temple of Mithras
Naples, 1998

The ruins of the temple dedicated to Mithras are located in the heart of Naples, in a zone of high density of construction, and are visible through a deep excavation surrounded by buildings. For this complex but highly unusual situation, a setting was required that would draw attention to the presence of the archeological site in a suitable way.

The proposal of a garden suspended above the excavation stemmed from the idea of creating a natural oasis amidst the chaos of the city and underlining, through a gesture of the sort made by Land Art, the presence of the past and the riches concealed in the depths of the earth in this city. A series of ramps allow visitors to go down from the level of this small garden to the ruins, observing the successive geological and historical stratifications that constitute one of the keys to interpretation of the history of Naples as they descend into the ground.

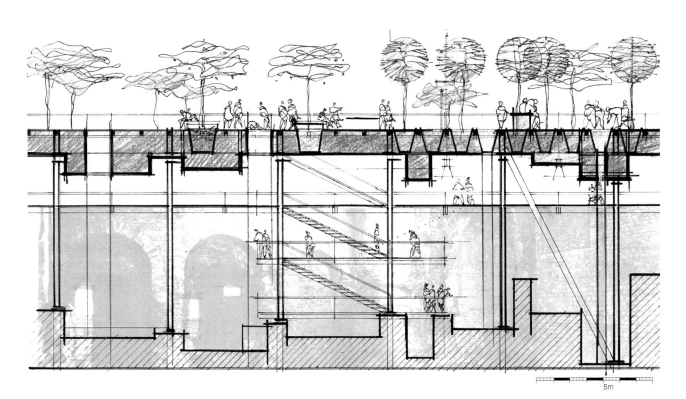

5m

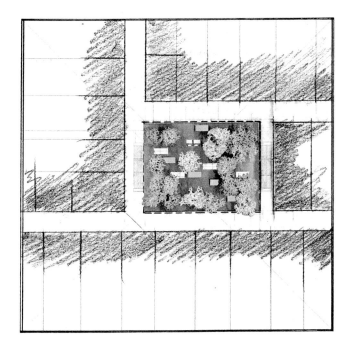
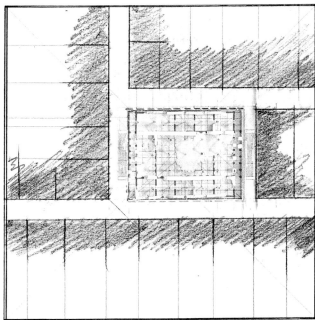

*Study sketch,
study section
of the structure.*

*Plans at the level
of the garden and
the sidewalk, view
of the model.*

Competition for an Urban Park
in the Falck Area
Sesto San Giovanni, 1998

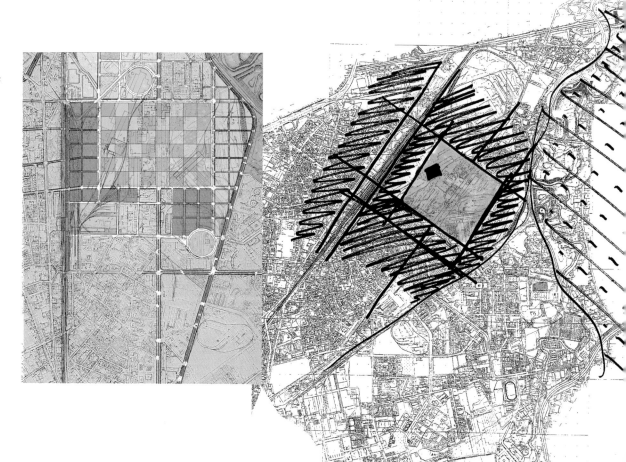

Promoted by the Commune of Sesto San Giovanni, the Province of Milan and the Falck Group, the competition of ideas called for the transformation of an abandoned industrial area into parkland for public use.

The basic idea behind the proposal was to create a park inside a town. So the first step was to lay out a grid of blocks within the total area (about 1,320,000 square meters) endowed with all the distinctive features of an urban environment—streets, public gardens, squares—in continuity with the surrounding fabric. The park is set at the heart of this new urbanization: a rectangle of 480,000 square meters subdivided into squares of 95 meters on a side.

The squares of this great checkerboard are planted in different ways (with evergreen trees, grass, shrubs or large flowerbeds), while preserving the existing vegetation. This choice is based on an interpretation of the site's industrial past and the intention to treat nature, in this case, as "construction material," arranged in patterns that bring out its intrinsic mechanicalness. The result would be a sequence of different landscapes, settings of Land Art that hold a dialogue with whichever of the disused industrial buildings it will be decided to preserve.

The identification and tracing of the grid would also make it possible to carry out the project in successive phases, with regard to the construction as well as the park itself.

*Study sketch
of the circulation,
location of the park
and the new
surrounding
districts.*

opposite
View of the model.

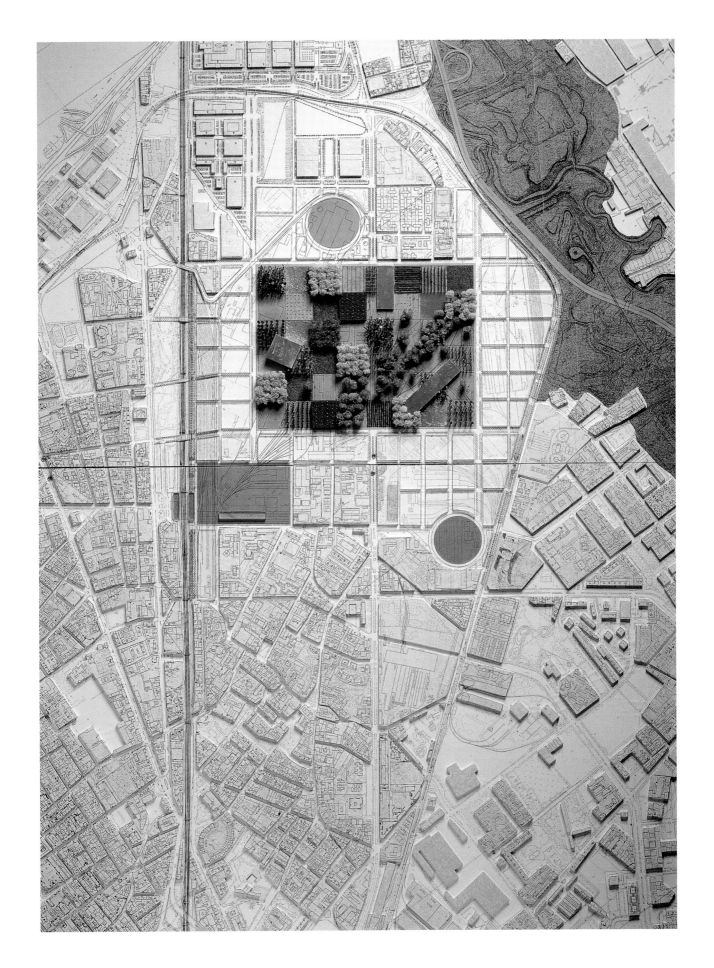

*Existing structures
in the Falck
industrial area.*

*Proposed layouts
within the park.*

quincunce
di alberi persistenti
di una sola specie

doppio quinconce
grandi e medi
alberi caduchi

C1   C2   C3

superficie   superficie
prato rustico   prato rustico

D1   D2   D3

linea   superficie   linea
arbusti caduchi   prato rustico   grandi persistenti
e persistenti combinati con qualche alberi   di due specie
                      radi

E1   E3

superficie   linea   superficie
prato   piantazione in strisce   prato
                      alternate di caduchi
                      e persistenti

F1   F2   F3

Via Bellini prolungata

Via Patranca prolungata

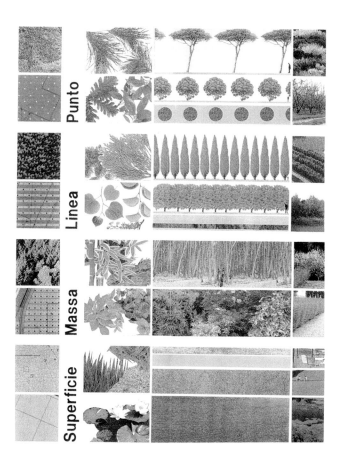

Punto

Linea

Massa

Superficie

opposite
Detail of the road system and the new districts around the park.

Proposal for the planting and utilization of the grid of the park, view of the existing state.

Competition for
Convention Center at the EUR
Rome, 1998

The program called for a commercial exhibition area with one larger space and three smaller ones, restaurants, cafeterias, a shopping mall, stores, offices, an auditorium for 2000 people and parking facilities. All these functions, which conjure up a hive of incessant activity, are enclosed in an extremely simple volume, a parallelepiped in which is set a large loggia facing onto the city, a glass box with a strong visual and symbolic impact. Three ramps lead up to the loggia from the square in front. However, there is also access directly from the street, on the main front as well as on that of the auditorium.
The internal disposition conforms to criteria of the greatest simplicity and functionality: the exhibition area occupies the ground floor, the loggia—a sort of plaza with stores and restaurants—the second level, and the auditorium the third. Although separated in this way, the functions are not cut off from each other, thanks to a carefully designed system of vertical and horizontal circulation. The layout of the individual levels is designed to provide the maximum of flexibility. The glass surfaces of the façades are differentiated to allow varying levels of light to enter according to their orientation. In any case, the overall effect is that of a living and pulsating volume in continual transformation, depending on the point of view and the external and internal light.

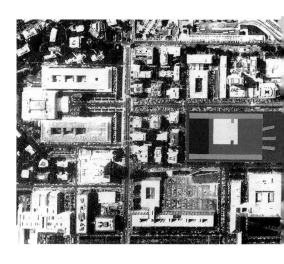

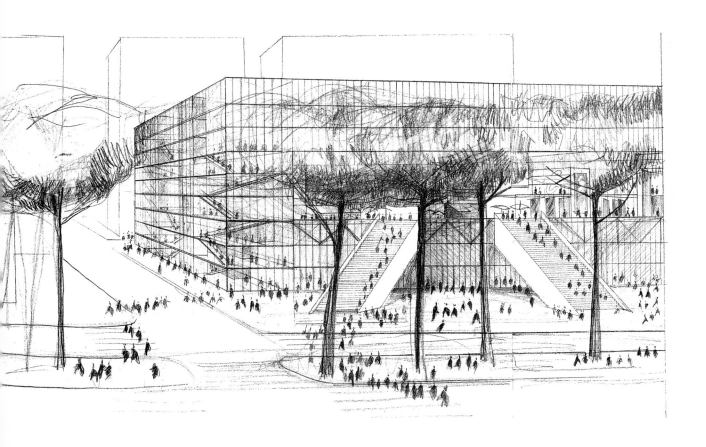

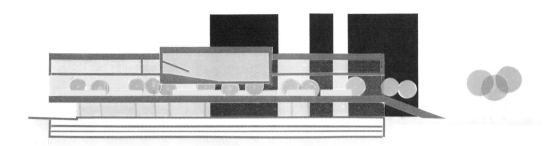

*Location
of the building in
the urban fabric,
view from the
access zone.*

*Lateral profile,
view of the model,
sketches of the
constituent
elements.*

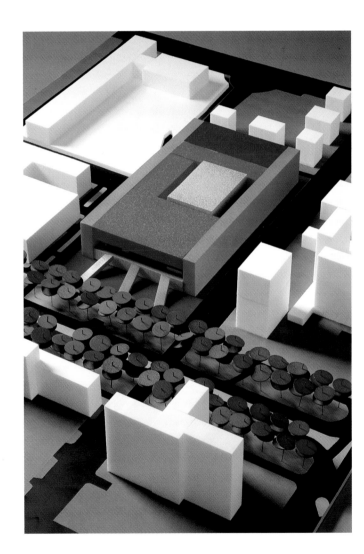

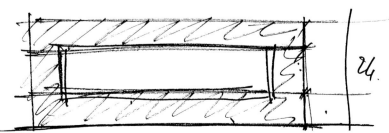

Competition for the Layout of Piazza Gramsci
Cinisello Balsamo, 1999–2003

The project is part of a broader scheme for upgrading of the center that will require a fairly long time to be realized. However, the decision was taken to make a space in the heart of the historic town available to the population right away, through an operation of limited cost that would be susceptible to variation over the course of time—as in the case of the traffic system, since for a certain period vehicles will have to go on using the square until the historic center is turned into a pedestrian precinct. Alongside these general lines, the solution proposed identifies the need to reestablish a special relationship of the public space with the church of Sant'-Ambrogio and its parvis, and to make it possible for the weekly market to be held there as it used to be in the past.

The elements of the project are few and simple: in the first place a copse of trees in a position diametrically opposite that of the church, so that they form the two poles of the square. In the second place, the raising of all the pedestrian areas and the covering of the entire surface with the same material (pale gray cement), including the reclaimed alleys and the streets accessible solely on foot. The urban furniture is equally simple, characterized by illumination from above along the main axis, with streetlights set on slender metal lampposts, and from below for the church and the garden.

Sketch.

Map of the existing state, proposed plan.

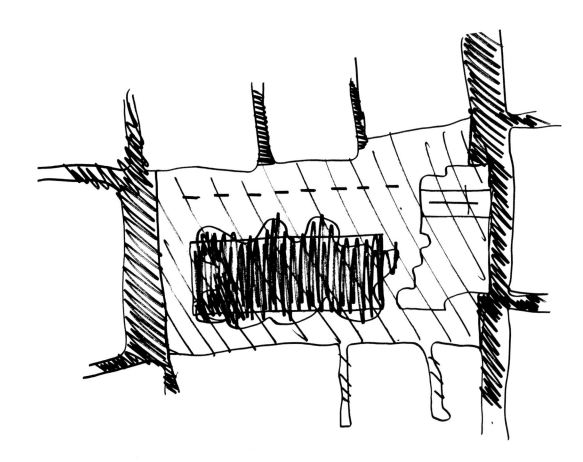

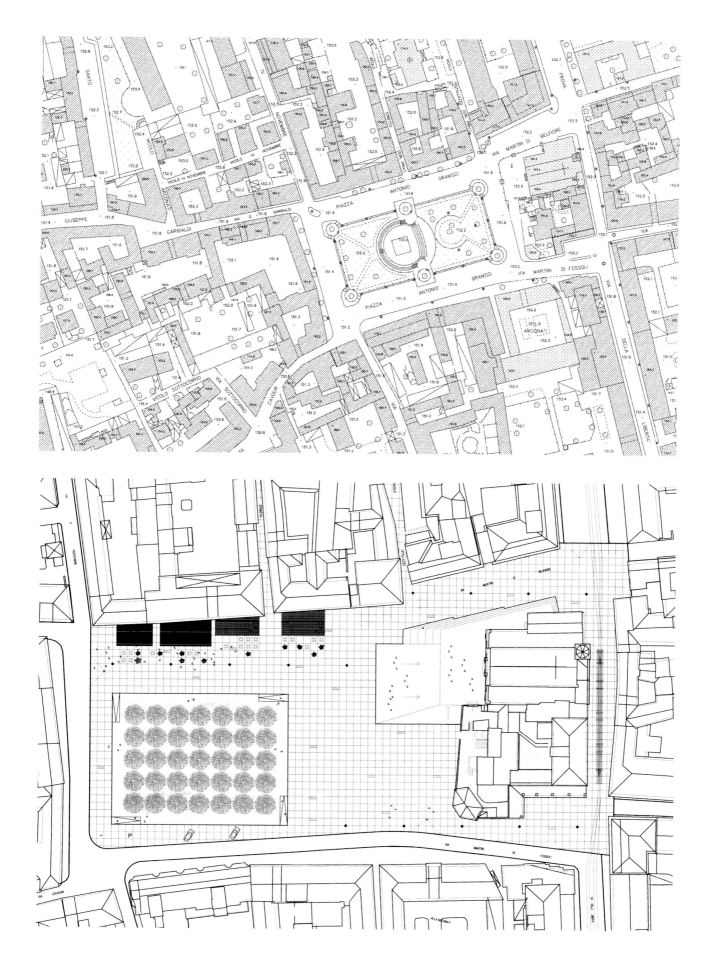

95

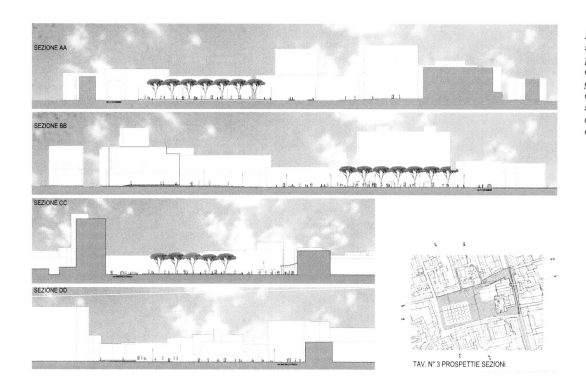

SEZIONE AA

SEZIONE BB

SEZIONE CC

SEZIONE DD

TAV. N° 3 PROSPETTIE SEZIONi

Elevations and sections of the proposal, view onto the new garden, view of the existing state in the direction of the church.

*The proposed
layout and the
existing state
viewed from
the church.*

Competition for the New Seat
of the University College of Architecture
in the Area of the Former Cold-Storage Facilities
San Basilio, Venice, 1998

The terms of the competition called for general indications to be used for the subsequent drawing up of a detailed plan for the entire area covered by the competition and the design of a new architectural complex to house the IUAV (Istituto Universitario d'Architettura di Venezia). This was to comprise a reception area and porter's desk, a multipurpose auditorium with a capacity of 500, subdividable into several halls, a conference hall seating 100, an exhibition space, a restaurant, a bar, a bookstore, teaching spaces with twelve lecture rooms and facilities for seminars, management and administrative offices and service and circulation spaces, in a total volume of less than 35,000 square meters.

The project proposed reclaiming the wharves, on which large slabs would be laid out in a checkerboard in front of the university. Public lighting, benches, kiosks and other elements of urban furniture will be set on this checkerboard. The pattern of the ground will be interwoven with the traces of the railroad tracks, which will be preserved. The buildings will jut out onto this checkered pattern that regulates the urban design of the constructed front. The urban fabric will be lightened to leave free open or covered passages between the warehouses.

For the seat of the IUAV the outer walls will be preserved, along with the profile and complexity of the building. The roof will be transformed into one of glass set on top of the existing structure. The glass roof will be covered by a mesh of copper wire to create shade and filter the light that penetrates the building. The copper will gleam in the daytime and at night as well, thanks to the light from inside that passes through the glass roof. On the side of the wharves, only one new opening will face onto the water, screened by an awning of copper mesh. The circulation inside the building will be visible through it. On the ground floor, the existing doors and windows will be left open or glazed, maintaining close contact with urban activity. Like buildings enclosed by a ring wall, the auditorium, the conference hall and lecture rooms will be organized like a small city within the city.

A bridge over the Rio di San Nicolò will connect this teaching section to the other parts of the university and to a bar-restaurant on the canal side.

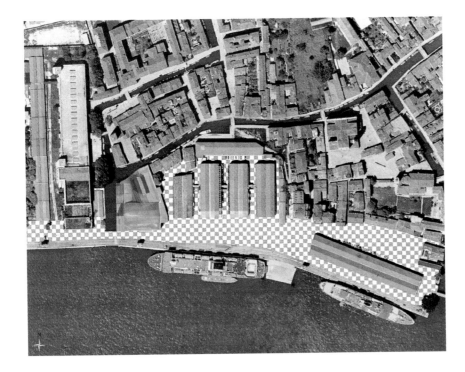

View of the proposal at roof level.

98

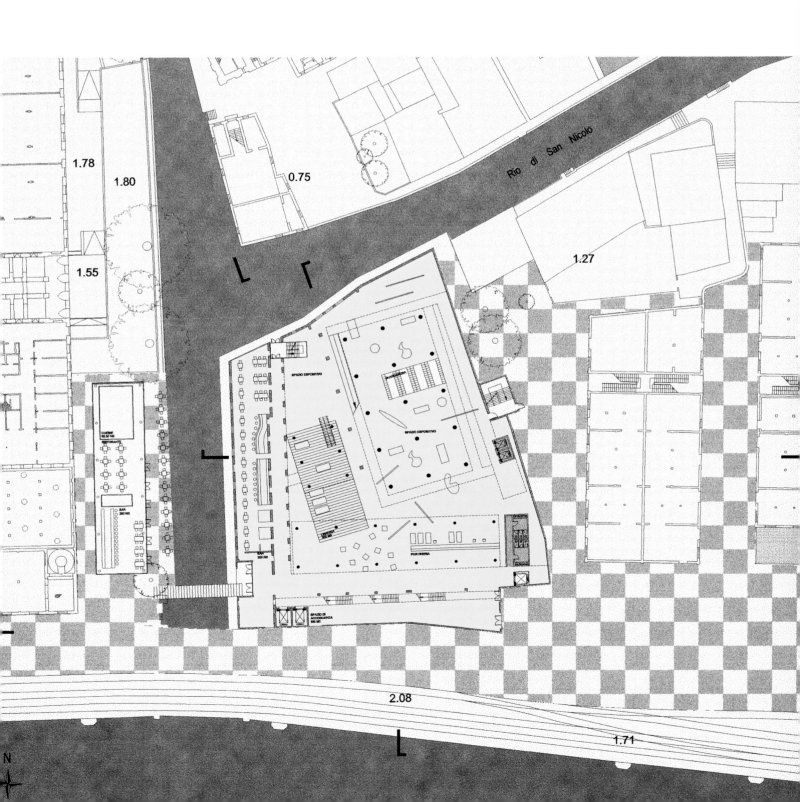

Plan of the ground floor.

Rio di San Nicolo

1.78

1.80

0.75

1.55

1.27

2.08

1.71

N

*Longitudinal
and cross sections,
the existing
sructures and
partial view
of the proposal.*

opposite
*Plans of the second
and third floor;
view of the model.*

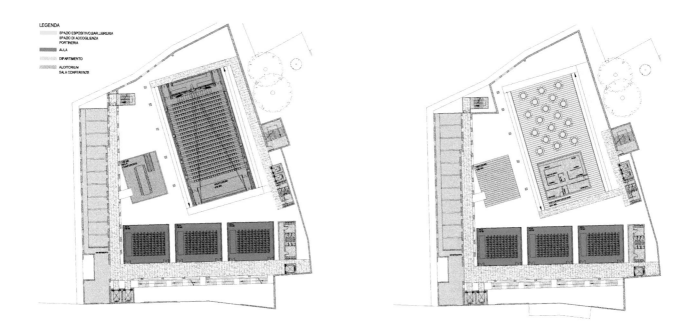

Competition Project for the Citadel of Justice
Salerno, 1999

The site chosen for the new law courts is in the quarter of the railroad station, and the creation of the Citadel of Justice should be the first step in a broader scheme of urban development that will cover an entire sector of the city. Faced with a program that called for 60,000 square meters of courts, spaces for the public, offices and services, the decision was taken to occupy only part of the large area available, opting for a high-rise building that would form a strong and representative landmark in the profile of the city. Thus the surrounding areas will be able to house future extensions and areas of public parkland. The complex is bounded by a set of squares arranged along a tree-lined avenue that flanks the river.

From the architectural point of view the building looks like a tower standing on a massive base that is tapered, creating a scale-effect first on the seventh level and then again on the sixteenth of the thirty-four planned, a disposition that corresponds to the various internal functions: entrance hall and main courts, minor courts and offices respectively. The "slimming" effect creates an orientation of the building with two different fronts, a narrower one facing the sea and a broader and more imposing one facing the river.

The curtain wall of the structure is made of black glass and white translucent marble, alternating in a pattern that recalls the pixels of a computer screen.

Planimetric study sketch, road scheme showing the phases of realization.

102

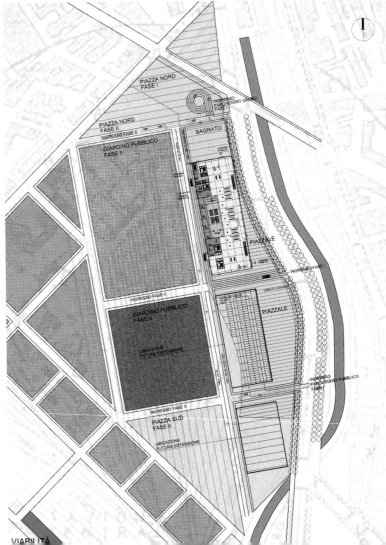

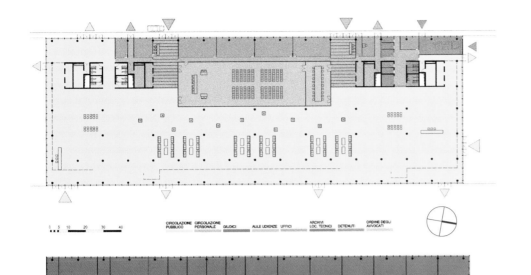

Plans of the ground floor and of the floor with two of the appeal chambers of the law courts, view of the complex.

CIRCOLAZIONE CIRCOLAZIONE
PUBBLICO PERSONALE GIUDICI AULE UDIENZE UFFICI ARCHIVI DETENUTI ORDINE DEGLI
LOC. TECNICI AVVOCATI

0 5 10 20 30 40

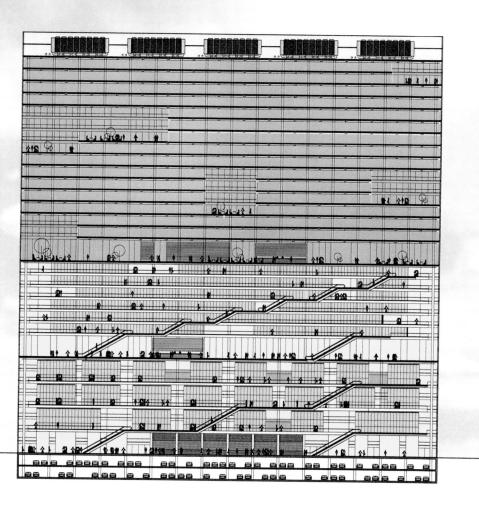

*Longitudinal
section showing
the coulisse and
interior view.*

CONSTRUIR UN PAISAJE.

UN BOSQUE Y UNA COLINA.

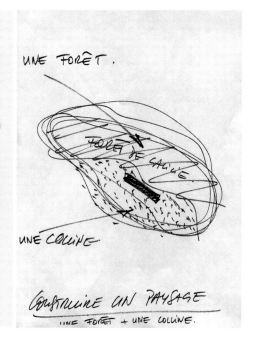

CENTRO HISTORICO / COLINA DE LA CULTURA.

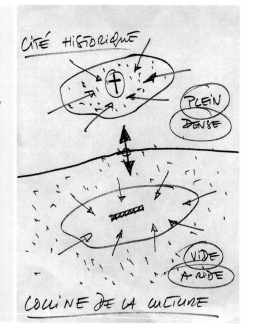

Illustrations
of the project
submitted to
the competition.

Location of the
project area.

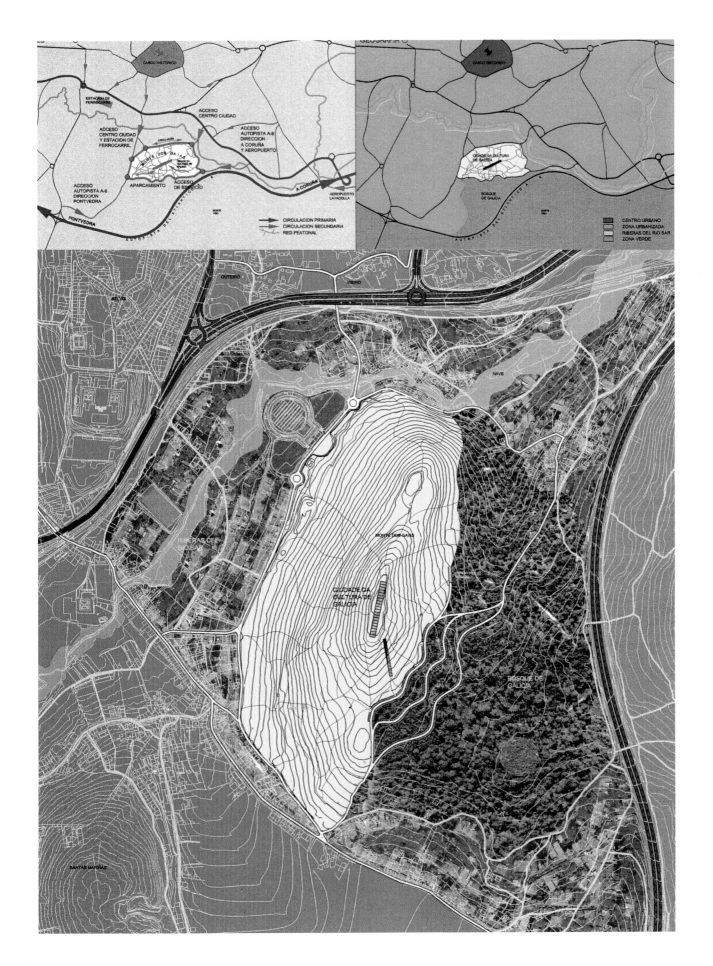

PLAN DE ORDENACION GENERAL.

LA COLINA DE LA CULTURA.

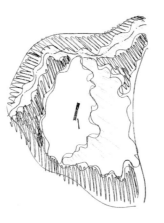

RED VIARIA

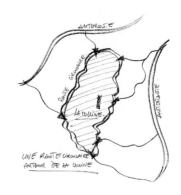

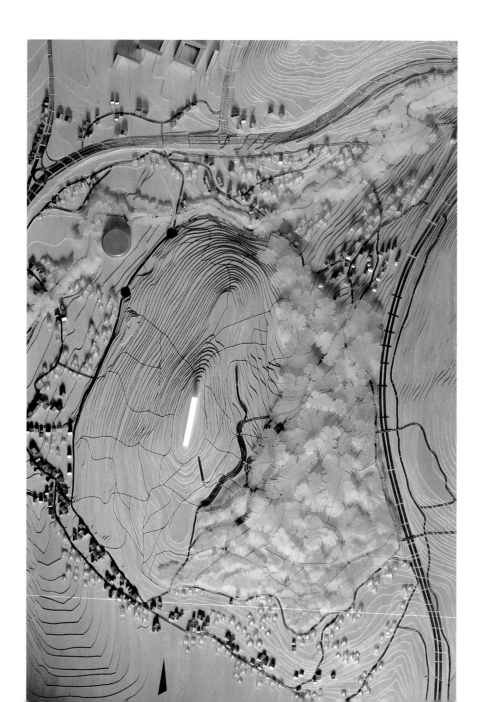

Illustrations of the project submitted to the competition, views of the model.

LUZ
DIA–NOCHE.

LUMIÈRE
JOUR – NUIT.

CONCEPTO
PLANTA /
SECCION.

UN
INSTRUMENTO
OPTICO.

**DIRIGIR LA LUZ
HACIA EL CENTRO
DE LA TIERRA.**

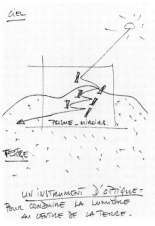

UN INSTRUMENT D'OPTIQUE.
POUR CONDUIRE LA LUMIÈRE
AU CENTRE DE LA TERRE.

PRISMA DE
LUZ.

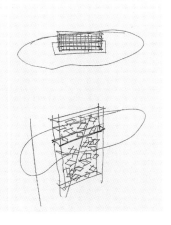

FASE 1 . SECCION = UNILATERAL

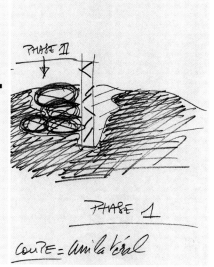

PHASE 1

COUPE = Unilatéral

SECCION VERTICAL

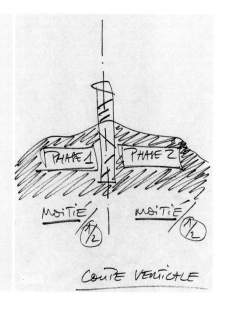

COUPE VERTICALE

FASE 1+2 = EN LONGITUD

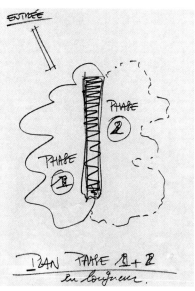

PLAN PHASE 1 + 2
en longueur.

110

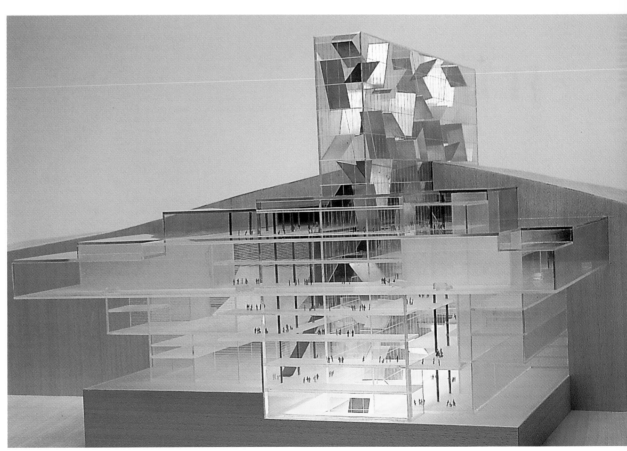

Competition for
the New Consiag Office Building
Prato, 1999–2000

The project, in accordance with the terms of the competition staged by the Intercity Water, Gas and Public Services Consortium, provides for the construction by lots of a single large, multi-functional building, surrounded by an extensive park planted with trees and well connected to the city.

The complex is divided into three main spaces, around which all the other functions of support required are arranged: bank, commercial spaces, nursery, restaurant, etc. Each of the spaces is designed to integrate with the other two, but is capable of operating with total self-sufficiency.

From the architectural viewpoint, the project proposes the preservation and restructuring of the existing pavilions, their structural consolidation where necessary and their modification to bring them into line with quake-proofing regulations. New structures will be added onto them that respect the inclinations of the existing façades as well as the roofs. A new structural lattice is planned to simplify the task of excavating beneath the existing buildings.

The materials are, for the most part, glass and concrete. Not wishing to carry out an operation of mimesis but to respect the preexisting structures instead, some walls of the additions will be formed out of gabions, filled with stones similar to the ones utilized in the original buildings.

The area between the pavilions will be covered with sheets of glass that can be screened with either metal grids or photovoltaic panels.

The presence of a large mass of trees in the surrounding park suggests the possibility of exploiting the difference of temperature between the parts of the park exposed to the sun and the ones in the shade to create natural currents of convection that will help to cool the buildings in summer.

The integration of vegetation and construction as well as the almost total preservation of the existing buildings, immersed in a transparent and permeable connective tissue of technology capable of interacting with the surroundings, are two essential elements of the project.

Model of the complex, sketch.

opposite
Main profile, plan of the ground floor, section through the common foyer, section through the exposition center.

112

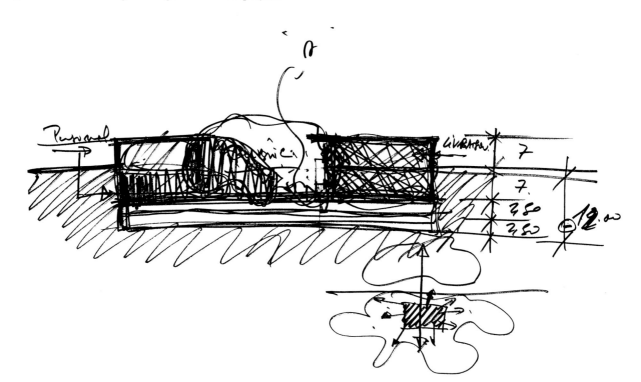

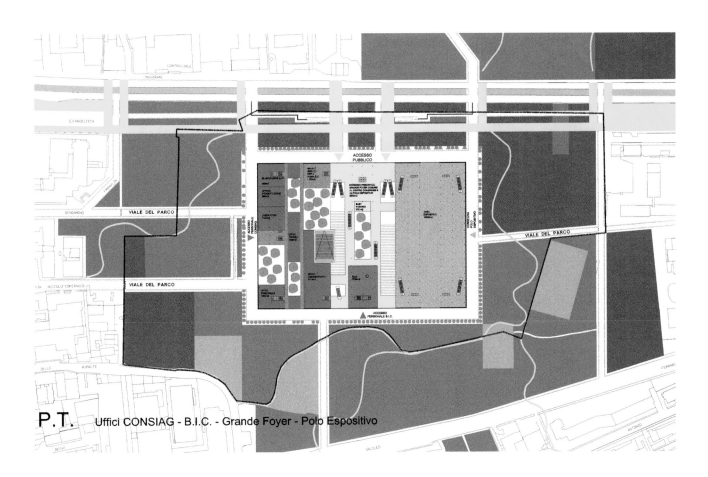

P.T. Uffici CONSIAG - B.I.C. - Grande Foyer - Polo Espositivo

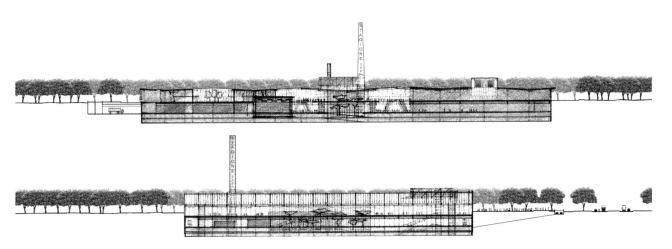

113

*Views of the
exposition center
and the Consiag
offices.*

Study sketch of the three main spaces, plans at the first underground level, the second and third underground levels, the second floor and the third floor.

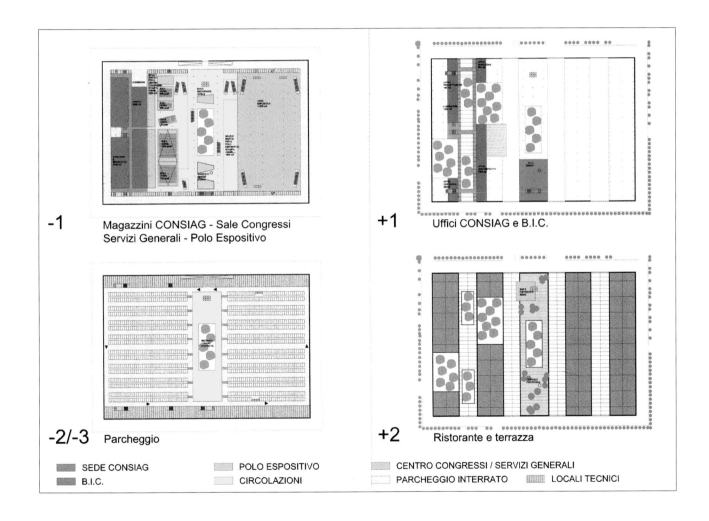

-1 Magazzini CONSIAG - Sale Congressi
Servizi Generali - Polo Espositivo

+1 Uffici CONSIAG e B.I.C.

-2/-3 Parcheggio

+2 Ristorante e terrazza

SEDE CONSIAG
B.I.C.
POLO ESPOSITIVO
CIRCOLAZIONI
CENTRO CONGRESSI / SERVIZI GENERALI
PARCHEGGIO INTERRATO
LOCALI TECNICI

M-Preis Supermarket
Wattens, 1999

The project is for a small supermarket, covering around 1500 square meters, of the M-Preis chain currently present only in the Tyrol region of Austria.

The site is characterized by two elements: the proximity of the crystal factory that draws millions of tourists to Wattens and the beauty of the surrounding mountain scenery.

To respect the landscape and to create a magical place with a strong sense of identity for the image of the chain and the city, we have realized an object of crystal supported by a spur of nature.

This crystal, completely geometrical object, meets all the requirements and functional needs of the supermarket; the spur of nature is the complete opposite, soft in form and natural in nature—birches and Austrian pines, like the mountains around. The direct natural illumination in the supermarket comes solely from this spur. This is the element that determines the direction and organization of the complex. This small fragment of nature constitutes the main façade of the building and is what characterizes it.

The diffraction of light through the other façades made of special glass, of a crystalline white color, brings a natural and filtered illumination into the whole of the supermarket, but above all obscures the views of the interior from the outside. In the opposite direction the views are clearer and allow perception of the surrounding landscape, producing an effect, a play of shadowy forms and light, by day and by night and permitting the use of normal and therefore economically productive fittings for a sales outlet, that bestows on it the enigmatic and scintillating image of a fragment of glass cut through the middle.

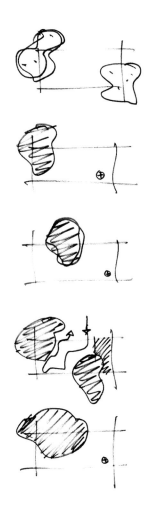

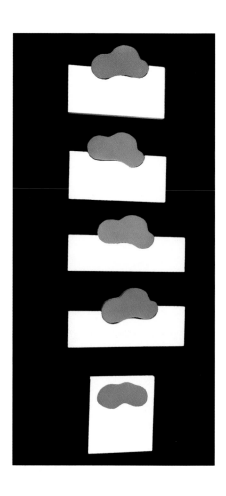

Preparatory sketches and study models.

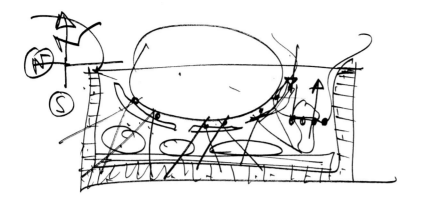

Sketch, plan
of the ground floor
showing the public
space of the
supermarket
around the garden,
delivery area
and storehouse.

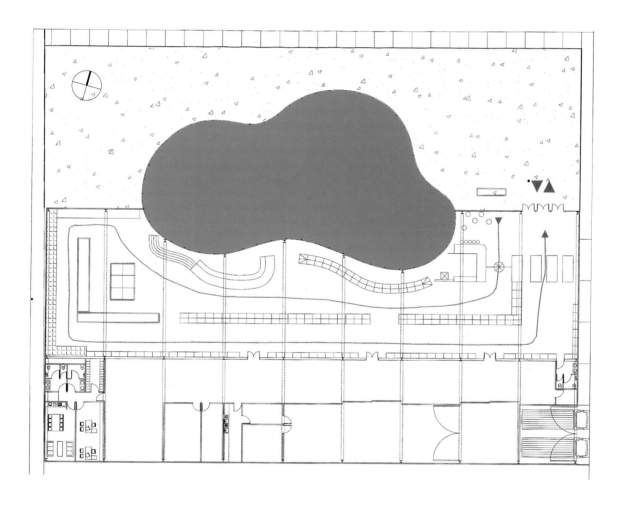

*Model with
and without roof,
elevations and
sections.*

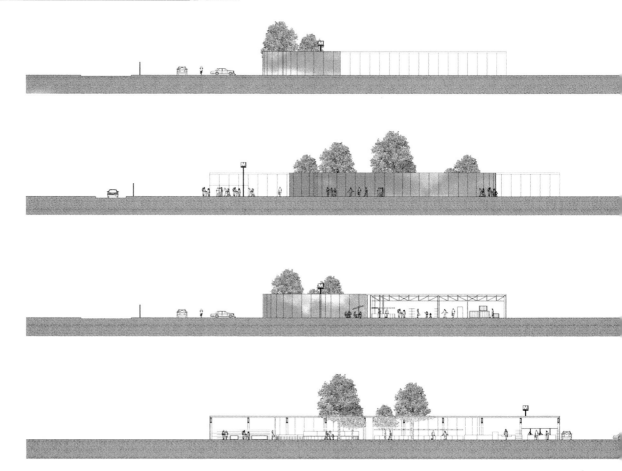

"Milano 2001" Competition
for an Illuminated Sign
Milan, 2000

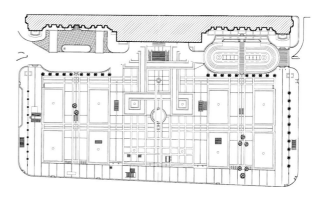

The project proposes a work of urban
sculpture, a gangway between two
walls of glass and aluminum, an illuminated sign to create a new entrance to
the new city of the third millennium, a
playful piece of sculpture that can be
walked through and that turns into a
beacon at night. An extremely simple
structure that can have a multitude of
uses: the screen for an open-air cinema
in the summer, the walls for temporary
exhibitions and many other things.
The aluminum structure supports slender elements made of unbreakable
glass. The same glass is utilized for the
elements perpendicular to the main
walls. They supplement the bracing provided by the structure itself. The inside
of the wall is accessible for maintenance.
The structure is permeable to the air.
The light sources, of an industrial type,
are fixed to the slab and are easily ori-
entated. Their light can be modified by
means of filters.

*Plan of the square
of the central
station, sections
in the daytime
and nighttime.*

opposite
*Daytime
and nighttime
simulations.*

Un segno luminoso : IL "METAFARO"

Verso la stazione - giorno

Verso la stazione - notte

Verso la città - giorno

La città - notte

Competition Project for the Enlargement of the Galleria d'Arte Moderna
Rome, 2000

The program called for the design of new exhibition spaces, an auditorium, offices, workshops and sorting and storage areas covering a total of 8000 square meters.

The project proposed the creation of a prism of colorless filtering glass that would also enclose the existing long sleeve. The addition has a lightweight metal structure, while the structural framework of reinforced concrete of the long sleeve is retained.

The façade proposed is made up of two elements of opaline, enameled or transparent glass, between which are inserted, according to need, panels of polycarbonate, Plexiglas, perforated aluminum or other materials that filter the light. These materials provide protection from the sun, fireproofing, thermal insulation and soundproofing, ensuring that the light that enters is natural, filtered, uniformly diffused and does not dazzle. The glass shell also covers the top of the structure.

It is proposed that the extension be built in two stages, with the construction of the head section with a second entrance gallery that also serves as an independent access for the auditorium in the first phase. This part is on three levels: the basement, accessible only to the staff of the museum, will contain a storehouse, technical services and plant; the ground floor is dedicated to the public; the second floor will house administrative offices and workshops, with access from the loggia for staff and for deliveries. The second stage comprises the extension of the exhibition spaces parallel to the long sleeve and its integration into the new building.

View of the present state and plan showing the proposed extension.

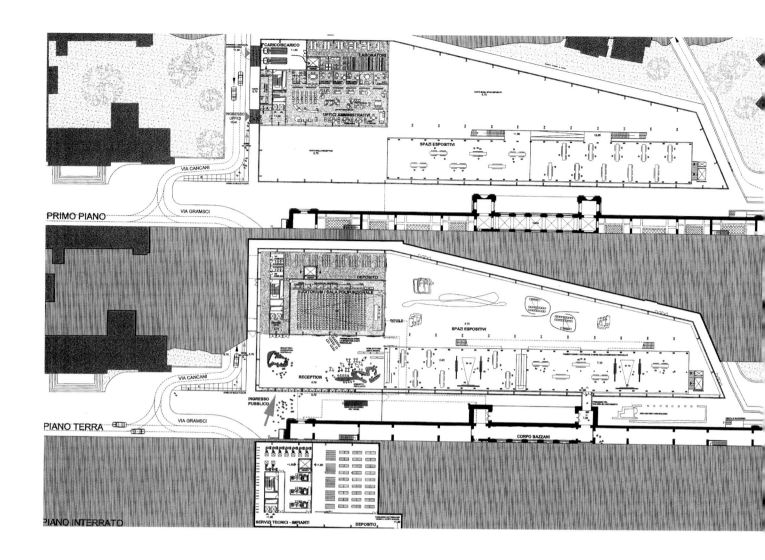

PRIMO PIANO

VIA CANCANI

VIA GRAMSCI

PIANO TERRA

VIA CANCANI

VIA GRAMSCI

PIANO INTERRATO

*Plans of the second
floor and ground
floor; model
of the extension.*

*Façades on
Via Cancani and
facing the Bazzani
block, longitudinal
section, cross
section of the long
handle.*

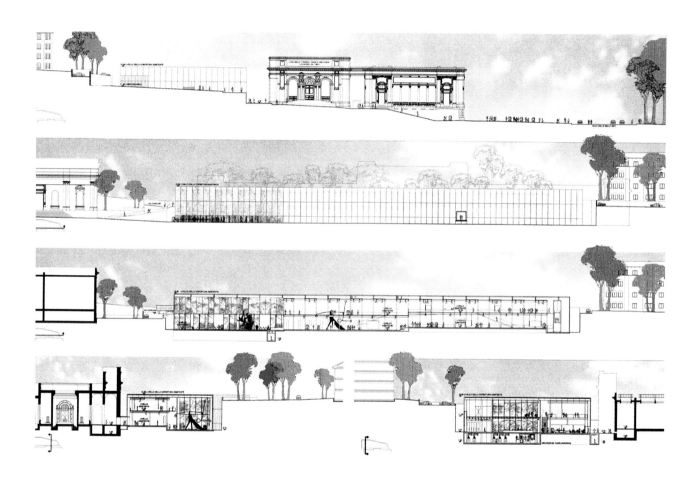

124

Perspective views
and model
of the proposed
intervention.

Design
with Gaëlle Lauriot-Prévost

Furniture for the Bibliothèque Nationale de France
Paris, 1989–95

① UNE CHAISE

② UNE CHAISE POUR "LIRE"

③ UNE CHAISE DE LECTURE

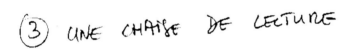

*Sketches and views
of the chairs,
produced by
Martin Stoll.*

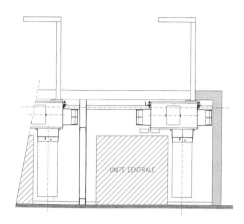

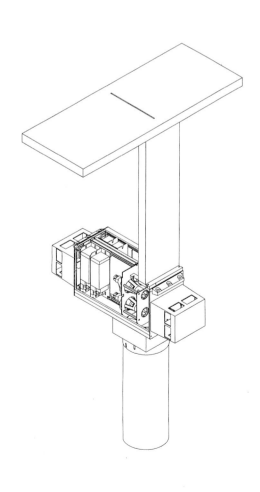

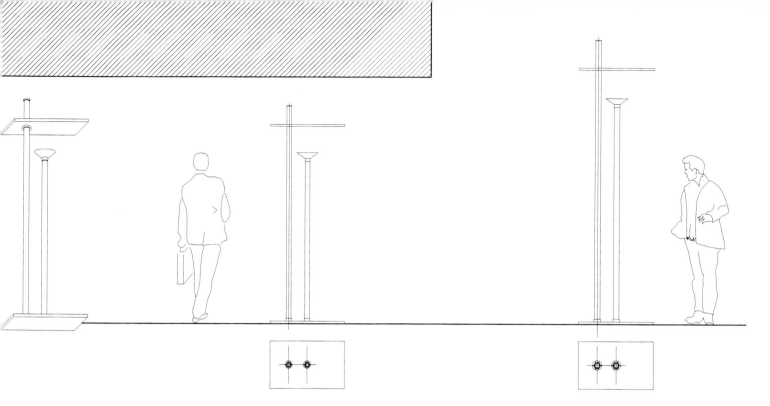

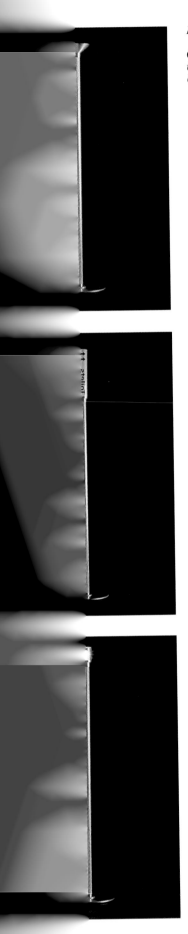

Lamps and signs.

*On the right,
the lamp produced
by Fontana Arte.*

Shelves and tables.

Metal Furnishings, 1999

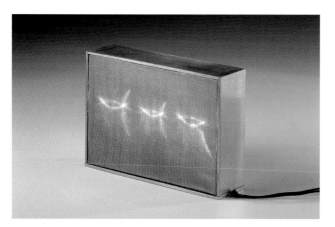 

*Lamp, folding
wire-mesh screen,
firescreen.*

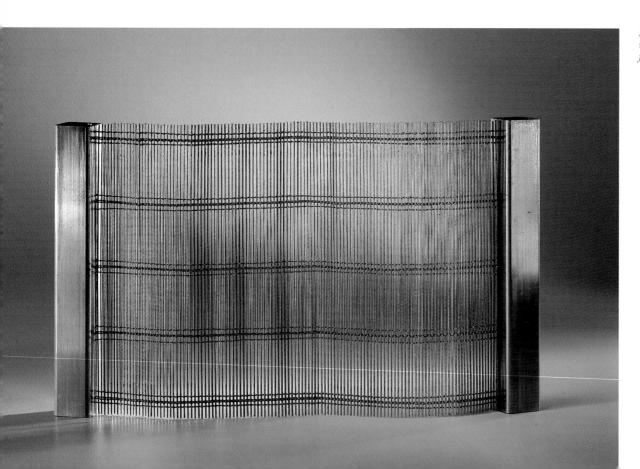

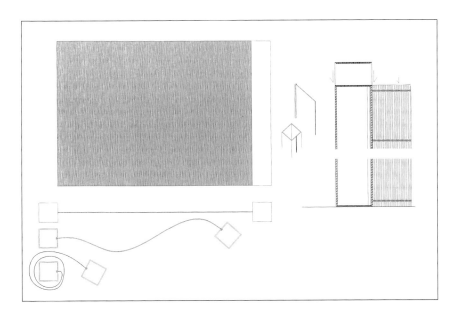

*Plan, section
and elevation
of the "Parafuoco"
wire-mesh
firescreen and
the "Case Candle"
and "Pleat Candle"
wire-mesh
candleholders.*

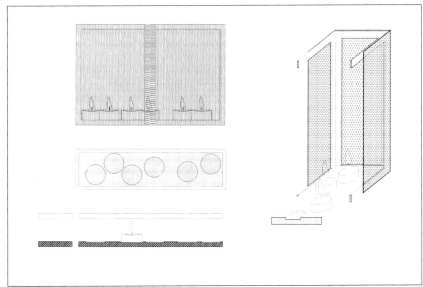

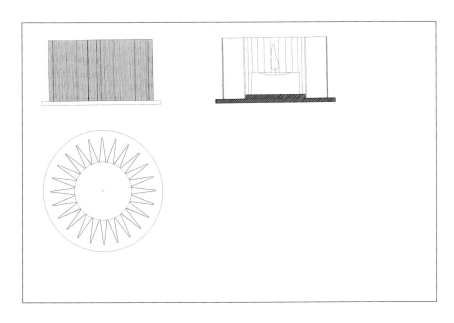

Chronology of Works

**Winning Project of the Competition
for the Someloir Plant, Châteaudun,
1981–83**
Client: City of Châteaudun
Program: machine-tool factory,
14,000 m²

**Three Apartment Buildings,
Rézé-les-Nantes, 1982**

**PAN (Programme Architecture
Nouvelle) XII, Trentenoult, 1982**

**Competition for the National Health
Laboratory, Montpellier, 1983**

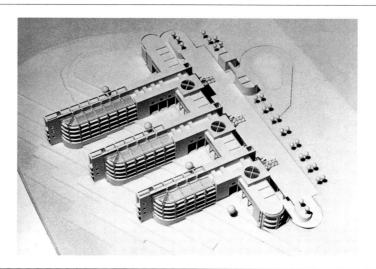

**Winning Project of the Competition
for the ESIEE, University for
Electronic and Electrical Engineers,
Marne-la-Vallée, 1984–87**
Client: Chambre de Commerce
et d'Industrie de Paris
Program: library, lecture theaters,
restaurant and kitchen, sterile rooms,
laboratories, workshops, gymnasium,
40,000 m²; for 1100 students in 1991

**Competition for the Seita
Distribution Center,
Marne-la-Vallée, Sector 3, 1984**

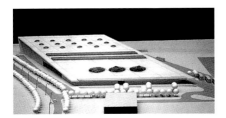

**Competition for the Command Post
of the Boulevard Périphérique,
Paris, 1985–87**
Client: City of Paris, Traffic Authority
Program: offices and workshops,
2200 m²

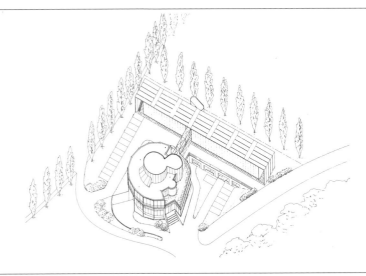

I2L Plant, Marseilles, 1985

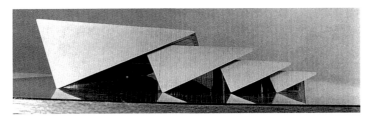

**Competition for the University
of Angers, 1985**
Client: City of Angers
Program: lecture rooms, university
library, administrative offices,
cafeteria; for 5700 students in final
phase; recommended project

**Competition for the European
Synchrotron, Grenoble, 1986**
Client: European Synchrotron
Radiation Facility
Program: tunnel, storage ring,
synchrotron tunnel, experimentation
hall, offices, service areas

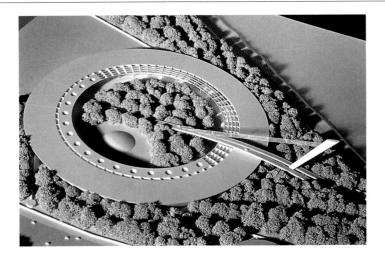

**Winning Project of the Competition
for "Les Cap Horniers" Housing
Complex, Rézé-les-Nantes, 1986**

**Winning Project of the Competition
for the Hôtel Industriel
Jean-Baptiste Berlier, Paris, 1986–90**
Client: SAGI, Société Anonyme
de Gestion Immobilière, Paris
Program: industrial premises, company
canteen, parking lot, 21,000 m²

see pp. 28–31

**Competition for the CFDT Bolivard,
Paris, 1986**

**Stag Advertising Agency,
Paris, 1986**
Client: Stag
Program: offices

**Winning Project of the Competition
for the SAGEP Waterworks,
Ivry-sur-Seine, 1987**
Client: Société Anonyme de Gestion
des Eaux de Paris
Program: renovation of the water-
treatment plant, offices, laboratories,
workshops

Metallic Fabric and Derivates, 1987
Program: study of products woven
or twisted out of metal or glass fiber
for use in architecture

**Project for Casa Mas, San José,
Spain, 1987**

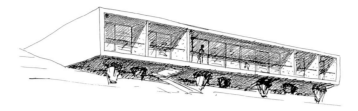

**Competition for the
Halle Saint-Louis, Lorient, 1987**
Program: indoor market

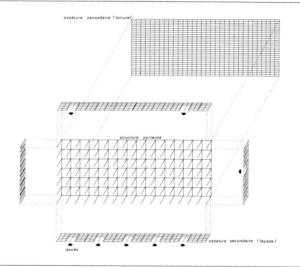

**Urban Development Scheme
for the Banks of the Loire,
Rézé-les-Nantes, 1987**

**Competition for a Methane-
Conversion Workshop, 1988**

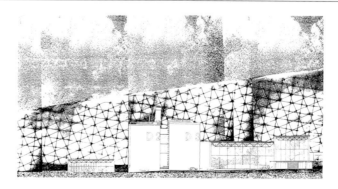

**Competition for Stand
at the Francis Le Basser Stadium,
Laval, 1988**
Client: Town of Laval
Program: stand with 7500 seats

**Competition for Ski Jump,
Courchevel, 1988**
Client: Town of Saint-Bon Courchevel
Program: ski jump for the 16th Winter
Olympics: scaffold, high ramp (120 m),
normal ramp (90 m), landing slope
and terraces, judges' scaffold, seats
for 35,000 spectators

**Competition for the Head Office
of the Newspaper *Le Monde*,
Paris, 1988**

**Competition for the Head Office
of Canal+, Paris, 1988**
Client: Cogedim Aménagement, Paris
Program: offices, broadcasting studios,
control rooms, computer rooms,
restaurant; recommended project

**Competition for the Pont Genty,
Paris, 1988**
Client: City of Paris, Traffic Authority
Program: construction of a second
bridge upstream of the Pont
d'Austerlitz, promenade, junction
of two stations

**Competition for the Lycée
des Biotechnologies, Nancy, 1988**
Program: training school
for the hotel trade

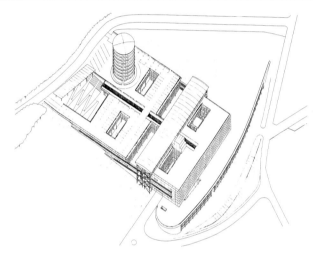

**Winning Project of the Competition
for the Housing Complex
of "Le Louis Lumière,"
Saint-Quentin-en-Yvelines, 1988–91**
Client: SCI le Louis Lumières
Program: 36 duplex apartments
(3, 4 and 5 rooms), parking lot, 4582 m²

Project Hysope, Paris, 1988

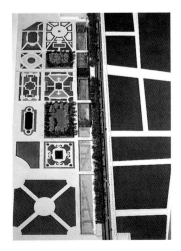

**Winning Project of the Competition
for the Seat of the Department
of the Meuse, Bar-le-Duc, 1988–94**
Client: General Council of the Meuse
Program: administration of the
department and General Council,
12,100 m²

**Competition for the Military
Hospital of the Armée Percy,
Clamart, 1988**

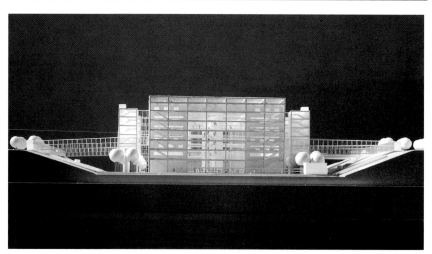

**Competition for a Sports Complex,
Sèvres, 1988**
Client: City of Sèvres
Program: gymnasiums for competition,
gymnasiums for training, changing
rooms

**Competition for the School
of Mining, Douai, 1988**

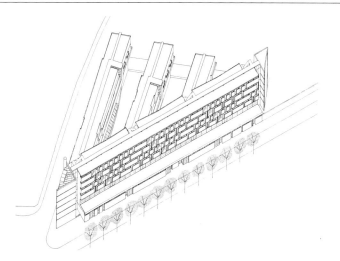

Competition for a Hospital Center, Albertville, 1988

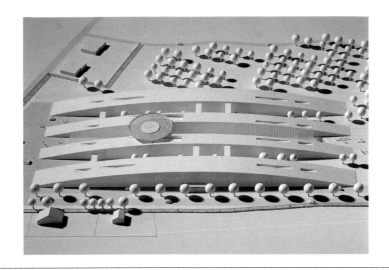

Competition for the CGI Office Buildings, Villepinte, 1988
Client: Compagnie Générale pour l'Immobilier d'Entreprise
Program: reception center at Roissy, four office buildings to let

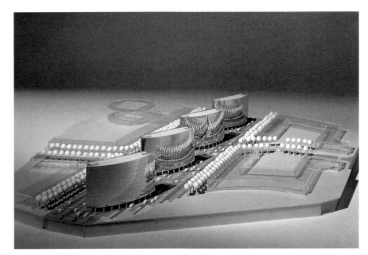

Project for the Croix Blanche ZAC (Zone d'Aménagement Concerté or "Concerted Development Zone"), Bussy Saint-Georges, 1989

Competition for the Head Office of the Technip Company, Rueil-Malmaison, 1989
Client: France Construction
Program: offices with space for 1600 workers, 70% in single offices and 30% in open space

145

Competition for the European Court of Human Rights, Strasbourg, 1989

Competition for a Technical College, Clermont-Ferrand, 1989

"Les Balcons du Canal" Housing complex, "Flandre-Soissons" ZAC, Paris, 1989–94
Client: Groupe André, BAPH
Program: 93 apartments, stores, 7000 m² parking lot

Competition for the ISMRA Technical School, Institut des Sciences de la Matière et du Rayonnement, Caen, 1989

Competition for the IFMA, Institut Français de Mécanique Avancée, Aubière (Clermont-Ferrand), 1989
Client: Ministry of Education
Program: research laboratory, lecture theater with 750 seats, administrative offices, classrooms

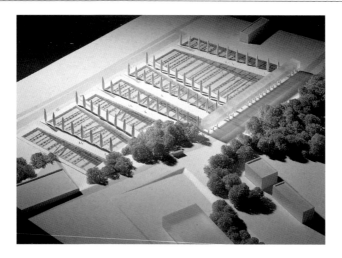

Competition for the Saint-Jacques Hospital, Clermont-Ferrand, 1989

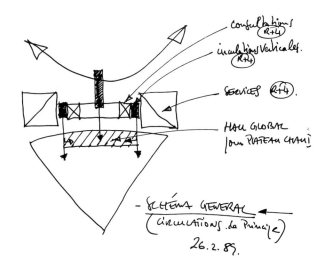

Competition for the Ecole Nationale des Ponts et Chaussées - Ecole Nationale Supérieure de Géographie, Marne-la-Vallée, 1989
Client: Ministère de l'Equipement
Program: ENSG: startup of the school in September 1991; ENPC: startup of the school in September 1992, shared premises: startup in July 1992; enlargement ENPC: administration, lecture rooms

Competition for an Exposition Center, Angers, 1989
Client: City of Angers
Program: multipurpose hall for reception with 4000 seats, catering unit

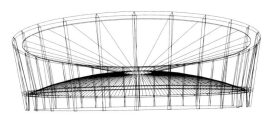

Competition for an Office Building at the Porte d'Italie, Paris, 1989
Client: Semapa

**Winning Project of the Competition
for the Departmental Archives
of the Mayenne, Laval, 1989–92**
Client: General Council of the
Mayenne
Program: reading rooms, exhibition
and conference facilities, offices
and storerooms for a total of 6000 m²

**Project for the Laboratories
of the Decaux Plant, Plaisir, 1989**
Client: Decaux S.A.
Program: management offices,
showroom, laboratories and
warehouses.

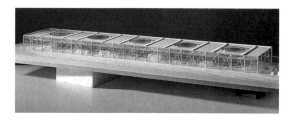

**Winning Project of the Competition
for the IRSID, Usinor-Sacilor
Convention Center,
Saint-Germain-en-Laye, 1989–91**
Client: Usinor-Sacilor
Program: exhibition hall, conference
hall, auditorium, offices, 4000 m²

see pp. 32–35

**Winning Project of the Competition
for the Bibliothèque Nationale
de France, Paris, 1989–95**
Client: Ministry of Culture
Program: reading rooms, storerooms,
conference halls, reception, offices,
350,000 m²

see pp. 36–45

**Project for the Tolbiac-Massena
ZAC, Paris, 1990**
Client: Semapa

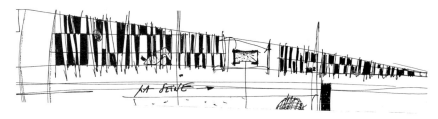

**Competition for the Niffer Basin,
Mulhouse (Rhine-Rhône), 1990**
Program: basin and harbor for
pleasure boats

**Competition for the Citis
Technological Pole, Hérouville, 1991**
Program: study project

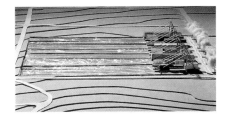

Denise René Gallery, Paris, 1991–92
Client: Denise René
Program: renovation of the gallery,
500 m²

**Project for Business Center,
Créteil, 1991**

**Advice to the Client for the Head
Office of the Alliance Française,
Singapore, 1991**

**Project for the Vitrine
de la Meuse in the Île-de-France,
Marne-la-Vallée, 1991**
Client: Ministry of Culture

**Domrémy Parking Lot, Paris,
1992–93/2000**
Client: Semapa
Program: parking lot with places
for 1000 vehicles

**Competition for Mining Schools,
Nantes, 1992**
Client: City of Nantes / DRIRE
Program: lecture theater, restaurant,
technology hall, lecture rooms,
administrative offices, residence
for 600 students

**International Competition
for the Lu Jia Zui Business Center,
Shanghai - Pu Dong, 1992**
Client: City of Shanghai

**Competition for the Layout
of the Banks of the Garonne,
Bordeaux, 1992–94**
Program: proposal for layout of both
banks of the river where it passes
through Bordeaux: foot and cycle
paths, cafés and small fixtures, future
streetcar route, parking lot; location
study for a crossing of the Garonne;
Coeur de Bastide ZAC: preliminary
studies, PAZ and RAZ, questionnaire
for public-opinion survey

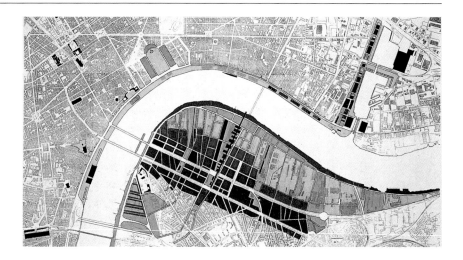

**Competition for the Layout
of the Place d'Youville,**
Montreal, 1992
Client: City of Montréal

**Winning Project of the Competition
for the Olympic Velodrome
and Swimming Pool, Berlin, 1992–99**
Client: Olympia 2000
Sportstättenbauten GmbH
Program: Olympic velodrome with
seating for 10,000 and swimming pool
with seating for 6000
see pp. 46–53

**Competition for Sulzer Installation,
Winterthur, 1992**
Client: Sulzer
Program: restoration of a complex
of industrial buildings owned
by the company

**Competition for the Wilhelm
Gallery, Potsdam, 1993**
Client: Deutsche Bank
Program: office building and stores

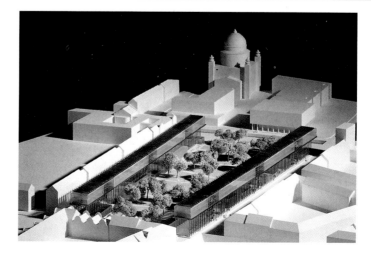

**Competition for the Neptune
Sewage Works,
Nantes - Petite Californie, 1993**

**Technal Stand at the Batimat,
Paris, 1993**
Client: Technal
Program: design of a 500-m² stand

**Competition for the Erol Aksoy
Foundation, Istanbul, 1993**

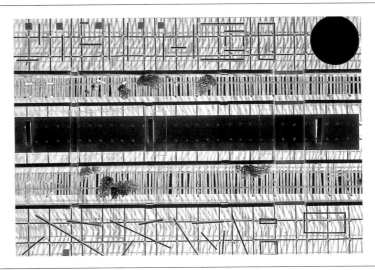

Centre Technique du Livre,
Bussy Saint-Georges, 1993–95
Client: Bibliothèque Nationale
de France
Program: workshops and storerooms

152   *see pp. 54–57*

Competition for the Restructuring of the Zoological Park, Vincennes, 1993
Client: Muséum National d'Histoire Naturelle
Program: restructuring of the park with new biotopes

Winning Project of the Urbanistic Competition for Le Grand Stade, Melun-Sénart, 1993
Client: Ministry of Youth and Sport, SAN of Melun-Sénart
Program: large stadium for the World Soccer Cup in 1998, 85,000 seats, 12,000 parking places for vehicles; training stadium; urban and landscape restructuring around the stadium; not built

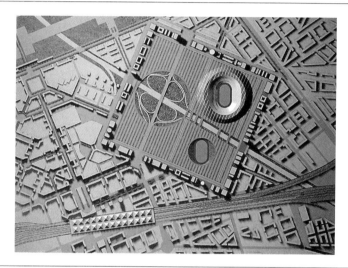

Villa in Brittany, 1994–96

Glass House, Düsseldorf, 1994
Program: research and exhibition
project for the International Workshop
"Architectural Visions for Europe"

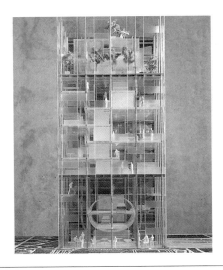

**Winning Project of the Competition
for a Savings Bank, Salzburg, 1994**
Client: Salzburger Sparkasse
Program: office building with safe
deposit and cash desk; not built

**Project for the Redevelopment
of the Île Saint-Anne, Nantes, 1994**
Client: City of Nantes

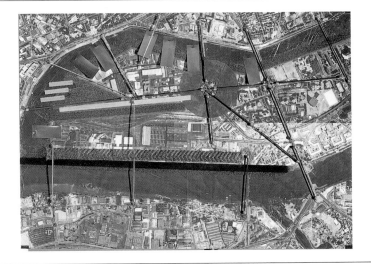

**Competition for the Hypo-Bank
on Theatinerstrasse, Munich, 1994**
Client: Bayerische Hypotheken- und
Wechselbank
Program: head office of the Hypo-
Bank, "Theatinerstrasse" scheme:
restructuring of a block in the center
of Munich to be used for offices, stores
and a cultural center

Competition for the International Terminal Port, Yokohama, 1994
Client: City of Yokohama
Program: building for embarkation and access to ships, stores, restaurants, galleries, reception and convention rooms; cited project

Competition for a High-Tension Electricity Pylon, 1995

ZAC of the Village of Lognes,
Marne-la-Vallée, 1995

Competition for a Building of the Ministry of Culture on Rue de Saint-Honoré, Paris, 1995
Client: Ministry of Culture
Program: renovation and new construction for offices, exhibition spaces, reception areas, meeting rooms, auditorium

Project for University Departments, Enlargement of the CMC, Créteil, 1995

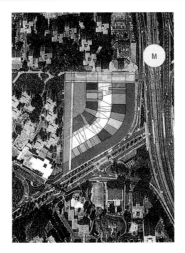

**Competition for Entrances
to the Subway, Berlin, 1995**

**Competition for the Brive-
Montauban Expressway, 1995**
Client: Ministry of Transport

**Scheme for the Restructuring
of the Storkower Strasse,
Margins of the Velodrome
and the Olympic Swimming Pool,
Berlin, 1995**

**Competition for the Plan
of Reclamation of the Unimetal
Area, Caen, 1995–97**
Client: Grand Caen District
Program: criteria for redevelopment
of the area; specific study of the
landscape, Plateau amusement park
and multimode services; preliminary
restructuring of the Plateau landscape;
prefiguration study of the Vallée
sewage works; study of insertion
of road system on the Plateau

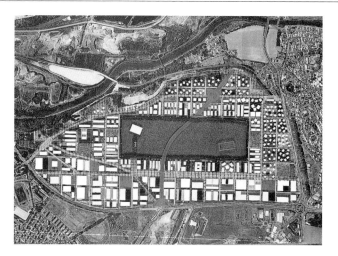

 see pp. 62–67

**Competition for the Place
des Nations, Geneva, 1995**
Client: City of Geneva, United Nations

**Competition for the Enlargement
of the Municipal Stadium,
Marseilles, 1995**
Client: City of Marseilles
Program: enlargement and overhaul
of the velodrome stadium
for the 1998 World Cup; construction
of a stand with 60,000 seats, 1,500
parking places for competitors
and guests; restructuring of the
surroundings

**HYMN, Project for Installation
of the Works of Francis Giacobetti,
Paris, 1995**
Program: intervention for the location
of an object in relation to its setting,
which is not modified but enriched
with specific and symbolic meaning

**Furniture for the Bibliothèque
Nationale de France, Paris, 1996**
Client: Bibliothèque Nationale
de France
Program: design of the 4000 public
reading stations including tables,
shelves, lamps and chairs

see pp. 128–33

**Winning Project of the Competition
for the Grande Serre, La Villette,
Paris, 1996–98**
Client: Cité des Sciences
et de l'Industrie
Program: 400-m² thematic exhibition
hall, 400-m² conservatory
see pp. 58–61

Central Stand for Elec '96,
Exposition Park, Villepinte, 1996
Client: Elec '96
Program: design of a 4090-m² stand
to display various light sources

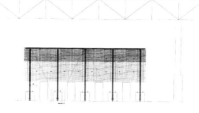

Winning Project of the Competition
for the Enlargement of the City
Hall, Innsbruck, 1996–2002
Client: City of Innsbruck

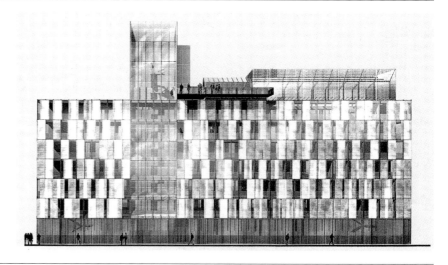

Competition for Urban Lighting
Systems, Paris, 1996
Client: City of Paris

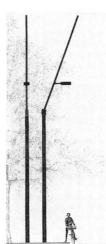

Kolonihavehus Installation,
Copenhagen, 1996
Client: Museum of Modern Art,
Kirsten Kiser
Program: a 4-m² "Kolonihaven"

Winning Project of the Competition for the Enlargement of the Court of Justice of the European Union, Luxembourg, 1996–2007
Client: Ministry of Public Works, Luxembourg
Program: fourth enlargement of the Court of Justice building, renovation of the old building, offices and premises for the presidency, members of the court and the chancellery, audience chambers, library, coulisse, restaurant

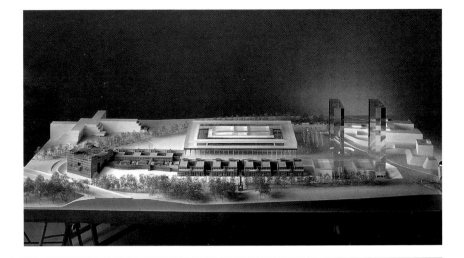

see pp. 68–71

Competition for the Archives Center, Reims, 1996

Competition for the Kansaï-Kan National Library, Kyoto - Seika-cho, 1996
Client: National Library of the Diet, Japanese Ministry of Construction
Program: storerooms, reading rooms for researchers, administration, conference halls, premises for various uses, technical premises

Competition for the Ministry of Foreign Affairs, Berlin, 1996
Client: Ministry of Foreign Affairs
Program: enlargement of the former building of the Reichsbank, renovated for the German Ministry of Foreign Affairs, with offices, archives and information center in the historic center of Berlin (Berlin-Mitte)

Competition for the International Airport, Dortmund, 1996
Client: Flughafen Dortmund GmbH
Program: terminal building and parking lots

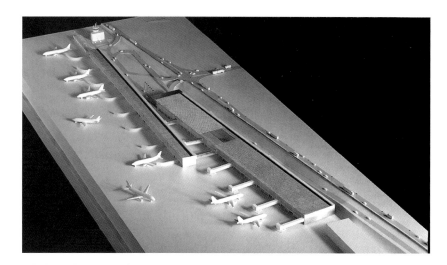

Competition for an Auditorium, Château-Gontier, 1996
Client: District of Château-Gontier
Program: auditorium with 500 seats; historic monument

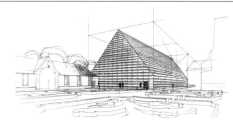

Competition for the European FedEx Center, Roissy, Charles -de-Gaulle Airport, 1996
Client: Paris Airports
Program: building for sorting and administration; airport handling area

Urban Development Scheme, Marly-le-Roi, 1997
Client: Town of Marly-le-Roi
Program: urbanization of a block and urban development scheme for the insertion of sports facilities

Competition for the Haute-Savoye Departmental Archives, Annecy, 1997
Client: Ministry of Culture

**Competition for Upgrading
of the Cargo, Grenoble, 1997**
Client: City of Grenoble, Ministry
of Culture

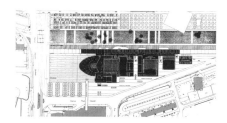

**Competition for the French
Embassy, Berlin, 1997**
Client: Ministry of Foreign Affairs

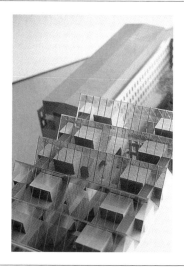

**Competition for Extension
of the Museum of Modern Art,
New York, 1997**
Client: Museum of Modern Art
Program: galleries for temporary
exhibitions, galleries for permanent
displays, conference halls, offices,
storerooms, conservation studio, staff
restaurants, public cafeteria, library,
bookstore

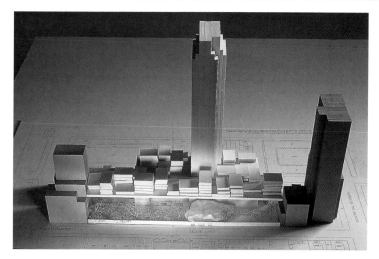

Security Policy Center, Geneva, 1997
Client: United Nations
Program: G.C.S.P. Institute, UN
training center with lecture rooms,
offices, conference halls and reception
areas

**Urban Development Scheme
for the Restructuring of the BLEG
Sites, Berlin, 1997**
Client: BLEG
Program: restructuring of a disused
industrial site

**Competition for the Olympic
Village, Kitzbühel, 1997**
Client: Town of Kitzbühel

**Competition for the Museo
Costantini, Buenos Aires, 1997**

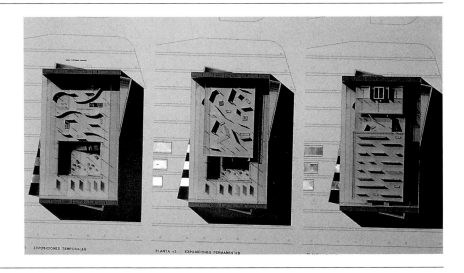

**Winning Project of the Consultation
for the Aplix Factory, Le Cellier-sur-
Loire, 1997–99**
Client: Aplix SA
Program: workshops for the
manufacture of tracked vehicles
covering 30,000 m²
see pp. 72–75

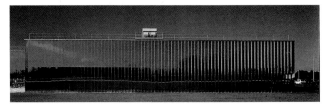

162

**Project for Three Hotels
on Guadeloupe and Martinique
in the Antilles and in Guiana, 1997**
Client: Gruppo Fabre Domergue
Program: study of insertion of three-
star hotels with 100 rooms into the
landscape on three different sites

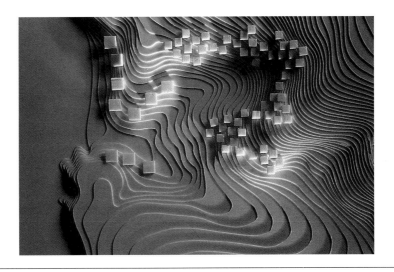

**Winning Project of the Competition
for the Mediathèque, Vénissieux,
1997–2001**
Client: Town of Vénissieux
Program: media library and services
covering 4600 m²

see pp. 76–79

**Bench-cum-Bed for the WANAS
Foundation, Installation,
Stockholm, 1997**
Client: City of Stockholm
Program: commission for an exposition

**Competition for the Layout
of the Place Roger Salengro,
Dunkirk, 1997**
Client: Town of Dunkirk

**Competition for the Upgrading
of the Area of the Tour
Montparnasse, Paris, 1998**
Client: Cogetom

**Competition for Exhibition Park
and Service Center, Basel, 1998**

**PO Box, Installation for an
Exposition, Villeurbanne, 1998**

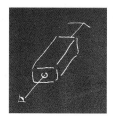

**Winning Project of the Competition
for the Lehrter Bahnhof Tower,
Berlin, 1998**
Not built

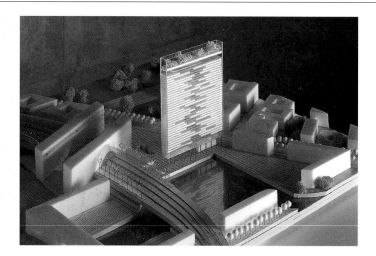

**Competition for Urban Layouts
Connected with the Streetcar
System, Bordeaux, 1998**
Client: City of Bordeaux

**Montigalà Sports Complex,
Badalona, 1998–2002**
Client: Town of Badalona
Program: training stadium and
changing rooms, competition stadium
with 8000 seats and urban layouts

see pp. 80–83

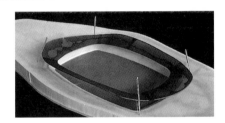

**Competition for the New Seat
of the University College
of Architecture, Venice, 1998**
Client: IUAV Servizi Immobiliari srl
Program: conversion of the area
of the former cold-storage facilities
into the new seat of the University
College of Architecture: reception,
auditorium, restaurant, lecture rooms
and seminar halls; harbor station;
building for administrative and
cultural use; bridge for vehicles over
the Rio San Nicolò, footbridges; layout
of the wharf on the Giudecca Canal

see pp. 98–101

**Competition for the Harbor Station
for Corsica, Marseilles, 1998**
Client: City of Marseilles

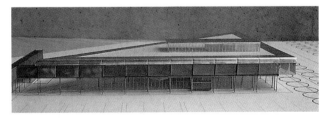

**Competition for the Topkapi
Exhibition, Versailles, 1998**
Client: AFAA / EP, Musée du Domaine
National de Versailles
Program: design of display structures
for the collections from the Topkapi
Palace in Istanbul, April–May 1999

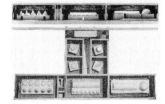

**Landscaping Project for
the Temple of Mithras, Naples, 1998**
Client: City of Naples
Program: enhancement of the ruins
of the temple of Mithras in the center
of Naples

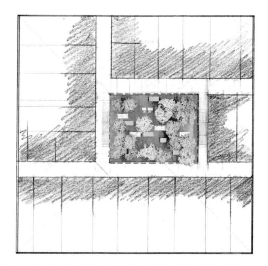

see pp. 84–85

**Competition for the Bercy-Tolbiac
Park Footbridge, Paris, 1998**
Client: City of Paris

**Competition for Upgrading
of the Central Market, Nancy, 1998**
Client: City of Nancy

**Pfleiderer Pavilion, Bau '99,
Munich, 1998**
Client: Pfleiderer
Program: construction of a 10-m^3
pavilion on the theme of technology
out of materials produced by the
company

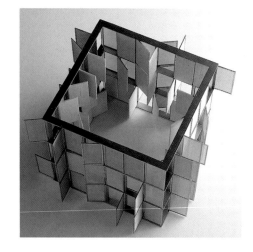

**Competition for an Urban Park
in the Falck Area, Sesto San
Giovanni, 1998**
Client: Falck SA
Program: project for an urban park
on a lot comprising the site of the
former Falck works

see pp. 86–91

**Competition for a Four-Star Hotel
in the Nahuel Huapi National Park,
Argentina, 1998**

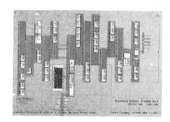

**Competition for Convention Center
at the EUR, Rome, 1998**
Client: City of Rome

see pp. 92–93

**Project for a Historic City-Plateau,
Luxembourg, 1998**
Client: Müller SA
Program: installation of the cableway
linking the historic center of the city
with the Kirshberg plateau and design
of the stations

Metal Furnishings, 1998
Program: furniture and articles
of everyday use made of metal
and wire mesh

see pp. 134–135

**Project for the District
of the Mediathèque, Vénissieux,
1998**
Client: Courly
Program: project for modification
of the land-use scheme

**Competition for the Design
of Noise-Reduction Barriers
for French Expressways, 1998**
Client: Roads Authority, Ministry
of City Equipment

**Competition for the Restructuring
of the Area of the Hôtel de Ville,
Marseilles, 1999**
Client: City of Marseilles
Program: Interior: council chamber
(hemicycle), executive secretariat of
the Hôtel de Ville, committee rooms
and offices; museum space; foyer and
reception, communal rooms; technical
premises; connecting galleries.
Exterior: layout of the squares
and the open space on the wharf

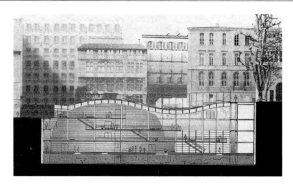

**Competition for the Design
of the French Pavilion for Expo
2000, Hanover, 1999**
Client: Decathlon

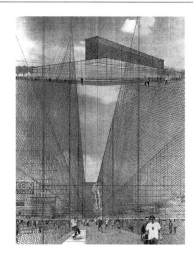

**Competition for Convention Center,
Graz, 1999**
Client: City of Graz

**Competition for the Layout
of the Station Concourse and Buffet,
Blois, 1999**
Client: City of Blois

**Competition for the Layout
of the Exhibition Center,
Stuttgart, 1999**
Client: City of Stuttgart

**Competition for the Casa da Musica,
Oporto, 1999**
Client: Porto 2001

**Winning Project of the Competition
for the Layout of Piazza Gramsci,
Cinisello Balsamo, 1999–2003**

see pp. 94–97

**Competition for the Citadel
of Justice, Salerno, 1999**
Client: City of Salerno

see pp. 102–05

**Competition for the City of Culture,
Santiago de Compostela, 1999**
Client: Region of Galicia, City
of Santiago de Compostela

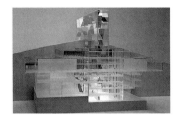

see pp. 106–11

**Competition for the Restructuring
of the Cognacq-Jay Hospital, Paris,
1999**
Client: Cognacq-Jay Foundation

**Competition for Enlargement
of the Museo Reina Sofia,
Madrid, 1999**
Client: Museum of Contemporary Art
Second prize

**"Tower Schemes" Competition,
Urban Layout, London, 1999**
Client: Tower of London

**Competition for the René Thys
Sports Complex, Reims, 1999**
Client: City of Reims

**Competition for the Consiag Offices,
Prato, 1999–2000**
Client: Consiag

see pp. 112–15

**Competition for Ski Jump,
Innsbruck, 1999**
Client: City of Innsbruck

**Installation for the Town Hall
of Brétigny, Brétigny s. Orge, 1999**
Client: Municipality of Brétigny

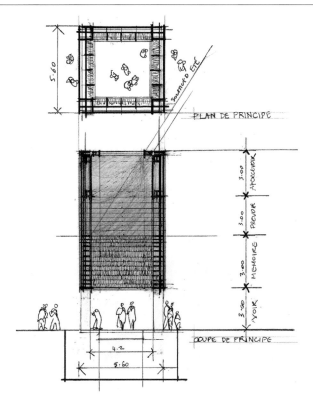

171

M-Preis Supermarket, Wattens, 1999
Client: M-Preis, Mölk family

see pp. 116–19

Grupo Imobiliario Habitat Tower,
Barcelona, 1999
Client: Habitat

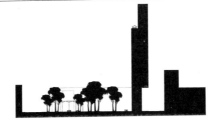

"Milano 2001" Competition
for an Illuminated Sign, Milan, 2000
Client: City of Milan, Arca

see pp. 120–21

Offices for the W.I.P.O., Geneva, 2000
Client: Ompi

Competition Project for the Italian
Space Agency, Rome, 2000

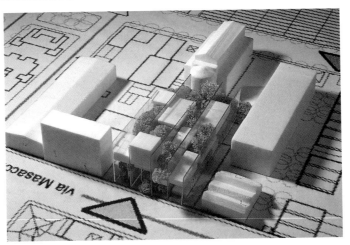

**Competition for the Stonecutters
Bridge, Hong Kong, 2000**
Client: City of Hong Kong
Program: 1000-meter-long suspension
bridge

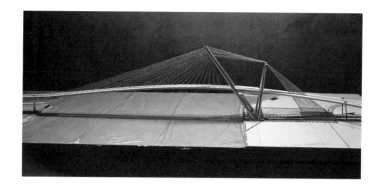

**Competition for Enlargement
of the Galleria d'Arte Moderna,
Rome, 2000**
Client: City of Rome

see pp. 122–25

**Haarlemmermeer Polder Urbanistic
Study, Haarlemmermeer, Zone
of the Airport, 2000**
Client: Gemeente Haarlemmermeer
Area: 55 km²
Program: urbanistic study, landscape
study, study of urban infrastructures

**Salhisaari Project Urbanistic Study,
Ruoholahti, Port of Helsinki, 2000**
Client: City of Helsinki, city-planning
department
Area: 70,000 m²
Program: landscaping and urban
study of new developments in the area
with 130,000 m² of offices
and services

Appendices

Biography

Dominique Perrault was born on April 9, 1953. He took a degree in architecture in 1978, in city planning the following year and in history in 1980.

In 1981 he opened a studio in Paris, followed by one in Berlin in 1992 and another in Luxembourg in 1999.

He has taught at the School of Architecture in New Orleans (1997), the University of Illinois in Urbana-Champaign (1998), the Escuela Técnica Soperior d'Arquitectura in Barcelona (1999) and the Ecole Polytechnique in Zurich (2001).

He has taken part in many national and international competitions, which have led to the construction, among other works, of the new Bibliothèque Nationale de France and the velodrome and Olympic swimming pools in Berlin, along with buildings used for teaching, housing, industry and administration and convention centers. Currently in the course of design or construction are projects for the enlargement of the European Court of Justice, for the Mediathèque at Vénissieux, for the stadium of Montigalà and for municipal build-ings in Innsbruck, as well as others of an urbanistic nature. In this field, for example, he has drawn up schemes for Nantes, Bordeaux, Berlin and Caen and served as a consultant to public planning authorities. He is currently adviser to the mayor of Barcelona.

He is also active in the field of furniture design and the study of new construction materials.

Among other awards, he has received the Grand Prix National d'Architecture (1993), the prizes of the Mies van der Rohe Foundation and the European Parliament for the Bibliothèque Nationale de France (1997) and the second "Deutscher Preis Architektur" for the velodrome in Berlin. He is a chevalier of the Légion d'Honneur, an honorary member of the Association of German Architects and president of the Institut Français d'Architecture.

Exhibitions of his projects have been staged in Paris, Bordeaux, Berlin, Lucerne, Venice, Copenhagen, Rotterdam, Barcelona, Tokyo, Lisbon, Stockholm, Innsbruck, Madrid, Tallinn and Helsinki.

Bibliography

Hubert Tonka, *ESIEE, Marne-la-Vallée*, photographs by Georges Fessy, "Etat d'architecture" series, Champ Vallon, Seyssel 1988, republished by Editions du Demi-Cercle, Paris 1990.

Bibliothèque Nationale de France, *Premiers volumes*, IFA/Carte secrète, Paris/Rome 1989.

Hubert Tonka, *Hôtel industriel, Paris treizième arrondissement*, photographs by Georges Fessy, "Architecture & Cie / Etat & lieux" series, Editions du Demi-Cercle, Paris 1990.

Hubert Tonka and Jeanne-Marie Sens, *Hôtel industriel Berlier*, photographs by Marcus Robinson, "La figure et le lieu" series, Pandora, Paris 1991.

Dominique Perrault, *Gros Plan 11*, Pandora/IFA, Paris 1991.

Dominique Perrault, *Berlin*, Birkhäuser, Basel 1993.

"Bibliothèque nationale de France," in *Vis à Vis*, special edition, spring 1995.

Bibliothèque nationale de France, 1989–1995, Dominique Perrault, architecte, Arc en Rêve/Birkhäuser, Bordeaux/Basel 1995.

"Bibliothèque nationale de France," in *Connaissances des Arts*, special edition, Société Française de Promotion Artistique, Paris 1996.

Dominique Perrault, Sens & Tonka, Berlin/Paris 1996.

Dominique Perrault, des natures, Architekturgalerie Luzern, Birkhäuser, Lucerne/Basel 1996.

Velodrome and Swimming Hall, OSB Sportstättenbauten GmbH, Berlin 1995.

Le mobilier de la Bibliothèque nationale de France, Sens & Tonka, Paris 1996.

Meubles et Tapisseries, Furniture and Fabrics, Möbel und Wandbehänge, Dominique Perrault and Gaëlle Lauriot-Prévost, Birkhäuser, Basel 1997.

Small scale – pequeña escala, Dominique Perrault, Gustavo Gili, Barcelona 1998.

L'Hôpital du Livre – Centre technique de la Bibliothèque nationale de France, "parole A" series, Sens & Tonka, Paris 1998.

Dominique Perrault, *Des Natures*, catalogue of the exhibition at the TN Probe gallery in Tokyo, Masayuki Fuchigami, Tokyo 1998.

I Dominique Perrault Sted, Eric Messerschmidt and Gilbert Hansen (eds.), catalogue of the exhibition at the Danish Architecture Center in Copenhagen, Copenhagen 1998.

Dominique Perrault, *WITH*, monograph, ACTAR, Barcelona 1999.

Claude Rutault, catalogue of the "Claude Rutault" installation at the Hôtel Industriel Jean-Baptiste Berlier, Paris 2000.

Velodrome, Landsberger Allee, Berlin, Die Neuen Architekturführer no. 22, Stadtwandel Verlag, Germany 2000.

Swimmingpool, Landsbergerallee, Berlin, Die Neuen Architekturführer no. 23, Stadtwandel Verlag, Germany 2000.

Composition of the Studio
Dominique Perrault, Architect

References

Dominique Perrault
Architect and City Planner

Aude Perrault, Architect
Administrative and Financial Manager

Gaëlle Lauriot-Prévost, *Architect-Designer*
Artistic Director

Associated Architects
Rolf Reichert, *Germany*
APP Berlin, *Germany*
R.P.M., *Munich*
Paczowski & Fritsch, *Luxembourg*
Luca Bergo, *Italy*
Joan Carles Navarro & Albert Salazar,
Spain

Technical Specialists
Guy Morisseau, ECAM
Engineer and Technical Director
Fabrice Bougon
Accountant
Jean-Paul Lamoureux
Acoustic and Lighting Engineer
Erik Jacobsen
*Engineer, Agronomist and Landscape
Architect*

Paris Studio

Architects
Constantino Coursaris
Ralf Lavedag
Natalie Plagaro-Cowee
Mathias Fritsch
Cyril Lancelin
Jerôme Thibault
Moreno Maconi
Anne Speicher
Thomas Barra
Katrin Thornauer
Severine De Love
Eve Deprez
Guilhem Menanteau
Thierry Louvriaux

Trainees
Yoel Karaso
Shigeki Maeda
Helen Brotschi
Francesca Rezzonico

Three-Dimensional Representations
Michel Goudin, *models*
Didier Ghislain, *elevations*

Secretarial and Administrative Staff
Sophie Dufour
Luciano d'Alesio

The publisher would like to thank the Perrault Studio for supplying the illustrative material and permitting its publication, and in particular Gaëlle Lauriot-Prévost and Natalie Plagaro-Cowee for selection and arrangement of the material and Georges Fessy, André Morin, Perrault Projets © ADAGP and Dominique Perrault for the photographs.

The publisher is at the disposal of holders of copyright for any iconographic sources that have not been identified.